THE SNARKY GIRL'S GUIDE TO BREAST CANCER

THE SNARKY GIRL'S GUIDE TO BREAST CANCER

Andrea Ciccocioppo Rose

Cover illustration by Amy Goropoulos and Paul Gingrich

© 2017 Andrea Ciccocioppo Rose
All rights reserved.

ISBN: 0692941592
ISBN 13: 9780692941591
Library of Congress Control Number: 2017913203
Andrea Ciccocioppo Rose, Mercersburg, PA

Statistics

"One day she finally grasped that unexpected things were always going to happen in life. And with that she realized the only control she had was how she chose to handle them. So she made the decision to survive using courage, humor and grace. She was the queen of her own life and the choice was hers."

—Queenisms

According to breastcancer.org:

- About 1 in 8 U.S. women will develop invasive breast cancer over the course of her lifetime.
- In 2017, an estimated 252,710 new cases of invasive breast cancer are expected to be diagnosed in women in the U.S., along with 63,410 new cases of non-invasive (in situ) breast cancer.
- Breast cancer incidence rates in the U.S. began decreasing in the year 2000, after increasing for the previous two decades. One theory is that this decrease was partially due to the reduced use of hormone replacement therapy by women

after the results of a large study called the Women's Health Initiative were published in 2002. These results suggested a connection between HRT and increased breast cancer risk.
- About 40,610 women in the U.S. are expected to die in 2017 from breast cancer, though death rates have been decreasing since 1989. Women under 50 have experienced larger decreases. These decreases are thought to be the result of treatment advances, earlier detection through screening, and increased awareness.
- In women under 45, breast cancer is more common in African-American women than white women. Overall, African-American women are more likely to die of breast cancer. For Asian, Hispanic, and Native-American women, the risk of developing and dying from breast cancer is lower.
- As of March 2017, there are more than 3.1 million women with a history of breast cancer in the U.S. This includes women currently being treated and women who have finished treatment.
- A woman's risk of breast cancer nearly doubles if she has a first-degree relative (mother, sister, daughter) who has been diagnosed with breast cancer. Less than 15 percent of women who get breast cancer have a family member diagnosed with it.
- About 5 to 10 percent of breast cancers can be linked to gene mutations inherited from one's mother or father. Mutations of the BRCA1 and BRCA2 genes are the most common. On average, women with a *BRCA1* mutation have a 55-65 percent lifetime risk of developing breast cancer. For women with a BRCA2 mutation, the risk is 45 percent. Breast cancer that is positive for the BRCA1 or BRCA2 mutations tends to develop more often in younger women. An increased ovarian

cancer risk is also associated with these genetic mutations. In men, BRCA2 mutations are associated with a lifetime breast cancer risk of about 6.8 percent.
- About 85 percent of breast cancers occur in women who have no family history of breast cancer. These occur due to genetic mutations that happen as a result of the aging process and life in general, rather than inherited mutations.

Preface

If you are reading this, you are probably scared.
Maybe you've recently been diagnosed with breast cancer.

Or perhaps you are a survivor, hoping it doesn't ever return.

Or maybe you are a support system to a friend or family member who is going through or has been through treatment.

In any case, you have a fear that lurks somewhere over your shoulder and every now and then – probably at night or sitting in a church pew – whispers to remind you that cancer has rocked your world.

It's OK. You aren't alone!

A cancer diagnosis is a life-altering event. It may not kill you, but it takes a shot at your sense of safety, sanity and self.

I will never forget the day I found out I had cancer.

I was shocked.

I was a healthy person with a fairly healthy lifestyle. I always loved me some sugar (OK, a LOT of sugar) and my exercise typically involved an occasional walk in the woods, but I kept my weight under control and didn't smoke or drink.

I had no family history of breast cancer.

I may not have appreciated it at the time, but I had been living the dream!

And then came the "M" word ("malignant" was the first word I got. Some people get the "C" word).

You'll find out more about my story as you read on.

But here is the "moral of the story" as a friend and cancer survivor likes to say every time she sums something up: As a person with cancer, you can choose to be a victim of the disease or you can choose to do the best you can to be normal.

I chose to be normal.

And, frankly, that was one of the most challenging parts of my cancer journey, because everyone around you looks at you like you are a victim at one point or another. You will see "sad eyes" and hear pity in their voices. Some of your friends and family may avoid you entirely.

I didn't understand that. And I didn't like it. So I began to look at the situation from a "snarky" point of view, hence the book you have in your hands.

You won't find sympathy here. You won't read words of pity.

I share with you my journey from my–snarky–point of view.

I will give you tips for getting along on your journey (or for being the support for someone else's journey).

I hope you enjoy it. I hope it brings a smile to your face as you relate to some of the things you'll read. Because in the end, that's what it's all about: enjoying your journey. Even when it's a journey you didn't choose … and even when it sucks.

Thanks for reading!

Acknowledgments

I am blessed. I know this. They say when you go through something like this, you find out who your friends are. I have been blessed with wonderful family and friends.

I list them here in no particular order and I hope I didn't miss anyone.

First, my boss at the time, Rick Cochran. Your kindness, flexibility and shoulder to literally cry on meant so much.

Dave and Donna Schankweiler and Larry Kluger. I thank God for you – and your health insurance. Your support and care inspired me. You allowed me to come to work after each chemo treatment (I say "allowed" because they could have insisted I take disability and made me fill out a ton of paperwork in order to work). That "normal" helped me more than you know.

All my JM colleagues, especially Amanda Bitterman, Megan Burns, Carley Evans, Amy Goropoulos, Amy Gulli, Aaron Hill, Christopher Hopkins, Ann Marie Irvine, Colleen Jones, Jennifer Neumer, Larissa Newton, Jillian Pavlick, Chad Pickard, Erica Reed and Hope Stephan. Thank you from the bottom of my heart for everything. You guys somehow managed to never change how you looked at me. You never treated me like a victim. You just kept working with me as always. I will forever be grateful.

Jodie Ruediger, my dear college friend, I love you for our Friendly's lunches!

Lauren Gross, you were there from the beginning to support me, make me dinner and do crafts to take my mind off everything. Love you.

Michelle Snider. How many friends would go and sit through four hours of chemotherapy with you? You are awesome!

Martha Howard and Elaine Livas. You gave me inspiration! I treasure our friendship.

Kurt and Katie Bopp, Sue Gladstone and Kathi Sites, thanks for being there from afar.

Tom Miller, of Massages By Miller, whose strong hands and chair massages always made my week. Thanks!

And I can't forget my new "cancer friends," Jennifer Bonnani, Dawn Zervanos and Michele Brymesser. Ladies, you are the greatest!

I also want to acknowledge Matt Nicastro and Ron Troskoski, my personal trainers. I could never have gotten through treatment and the challenges afterwards without you both.

Every medical person who laid hands on me (and there were too many to count), especially Dr. Leah Cream, Dr. Kristine Widders, Dr. Meredith Watts, Dr. Stephen Milito and Dr. John Neely, thanks for giving me my life!

To all those who prayed for me, especially my church friends and social media prayer chain warriors, I am blessed!

And last, but far from least, my family.

My ex-husband, Barry Ciccocioppo and his wife, Lisa. I know I was on your prayer list and you both helped Brooke get through this. Blessings right back to you!

I can never honor my mother, Barbara Quinn, enough for her support. She was there to take me to doctor appointments and dinner and beyond. I am truly blessed.

And my daughter, Brooke Ciccocioppo. What can I say? I live for you. You kept it together, never letting me see you scared. (Silly girl!)

And John Rose. The man who stayed with me (and married me!) through it all. You were assigned one task: keep it normal. You did your job and then some!

Thanks and blessings to you all!

Dedication

I've always wanted to write a book. I had many started, but lacked the discipline to finish. This, my first book (hopefully there will be more), is dedicated to:

My cousin, Robert Welker. Your voice has been nagging me for years: "Write that damn book!"

My ninth-grade Civics teacher, Wayne Cave. Your required essays sucked beyond belief, but they taught me how to write. Your encouragement over the years has been much appreciated. Blessings to you, my friend.

Brooke Ciccocioppo, I love you and adore you. You have become one outstanding young woman. Thanks for being my daughter and for your encouragement.

John Rose. I couldn't have done this without your support. Thank you! I doubt if this will prove to be a legitimate retirement plan, but the fact that it is completed is success enough for me.

Our Heavenly Father. Without this journey, I would have lacked many life lessons and blessings that followed. I always wanted to be published. Without this journey, I doubt I would have accomplished my dream. Thank you.

Contents

    Statistics ·v
    Preface ·ix
    Acknowledgments ·xi
    Quick Tips for Your Journey ·xix

1   Welcome to My Life · 1
2   A Moment of Fright is No Delight · · · · · · · · · · · · · · · · · 4
3   Tissues, Tears and Tenderness · 11
4   Another Diagnostic Test of Strength · · · · · · · · · · · · · · 15
5   Seeking Focus and Finding Faith · · · · · · · · · · · · · · · · · 19
6   Test Anxiety · 23
7   Life · 26
8   Getting Answers · 30
9   Off the Pill and Off the Rails · 33
10 Music to My Ears · 37
11 Sentinel Nodes and Surgery Day · · · · · · · · · · · · · · · · · · 40
12 Surgery day: Take Two · 47
13 Keeping Chapter 13 at Bay · 50
14 "Have you had any changes in your general
     health history?" · 52
15 "50 Shades of Gray" and Rita Wilson · · · · · · · · · · · · · 55

16	A Caped Crusader and a Soul Ride	57
17	Dark Thoughts and Low Blows	60
18	Help Me, Wanda. Help, Help Me, Wanda!	68
19	My Friends and Family Plan	71
20	Look Good, Feel Better!	74
21	"Obama" Joins My Chemo Administration	78
22	Chemo: Round One	81
23	Let's Talk About The Hair	87
24	My Chemo Journal Highlights	92
25	Sand, Margaritas and Nails	97
26	Radiation – Or as I Liked to Think of It: Snorkeling Practice	101
27	Speaking Out—And Falling In	107
28	Odds … and Ends	110
29	Finding faith	116
30	--30--	119

What No One Tells You · · · · · · 126
A Note to Friends and Family: Dos and Don'ts · · · · · · 132
What not to do: · · · · · · 132
What you can do to help: · · · · · · 133
End Notes · · · · · · 135

Quick Tips for Your Journey

If you are reading this because you have just been diagnosed or know someone who has, here are my quick tips:

Buy a couple new bras. You will want to buy new bras before you get a biopsy. Forget about an underwire for a while. You don't need that kind of negativity in your life now! Go cheap. Check the local discount store for soft ones that offer some support. No, they aren't lacy. No, they aren't sexy. No, they don't lift and separate. At this point, your goal is to keep the girls from too much movement and without a wire stabbing you somewhere. You'll need these during biopsies and beyond. I bought a multi-pack at a local discount store brought to you by the letter K. They hook in the front. They were the best purchase I made!

Be selective with whom who you share your diagnosis. You want support, not pity. You never know when someone knows someone who has died of cancer—and doesn't mind telling you all about that battle, even if it happens to be the same diagnosis you've been given. You don't need that kind of negativity.

Trust in your family. You will need at least one person to drive you to some appointments and to stay with you at some point. If you have one reliable person, great! If you have a few you can rotate through, even better.

Allow people to help you. When friends, family and coworkers find out, many will offer to help. Chances are, they won't know exactly what to do and you probably won't know what they can do either. That's OK. There will come a time when you need something. Don't be afraid (or too proud) to call on them. If someone offers, tell them there's nothing you need right now, but ask if you can keep them in mind for a future need. And then call on them when you need something. I thought I could handle my journey on my own. I couldn't.

Share your journey with your partner/those close to you. If you have a partner or a close family member, again, don't be too strong or too proud to accept help. I learned too late that I should have accepted help earlier in my journey. My logic was I didn't want anyone to feel obligated or put out. What I didn't realize was I was depriving those I loved most from doing something—anything—to help. It wasn't about me. It was about allowing them to be there for me so they didn't feel helpless. I didn't understand this then. I do now!

Accept the "ghosts."
You will have a few friends and family members who disappoint you. They may disappear from your life as soon as they find out. They may say nothing or do nothing. Or they may tag along on your journey, but hang at the edge of your path so that you know they are there, but they do nothing to help and offer no words of encouragement and, sometimes, serve only as a reminder that something is "wrong." I didn't find an effective way to deal with these people. I was very hurt at first and then I was angry. I finally decided to let go of my negative feelings and accept that these are the people

who simply aren't capable of handling a crisis. I just let them hang on the periphery. And they remain on the periphery today, sadly. As my husband says, just dial 1-800-LETITGO. It's not easy. But you have to decide whether to keep them or sweep them. And it's OK to sweep them.

Don't compare your diagnosis, journey to someone else's.
There is always going to be another person in your life, whether a friend, colleague or someone on social media, who has cancer. Don't expect your situation will be the same as theirs. You can hope it will be or you can hope it won't be, but don't compare. It's just not healthy. You are unique. Set your own rules and expectations.

Don't use internet searches! Put the keyboard down! Stop! Just stop! I know you are curious. I know you want to know about outcomes and life expectancies and the answer to some nagging little annoyance, but trust me, nothing good will come of it.

Scrolling down through Facebook? Reading a news website? See a story about cancer? DON'T CLICK ON IT! Don't read it. Just go right past it.

Odds are good it's a story about someone who died of the disease. (Doesn't anyone write about survivors??)

It will only send you into an anxiety attack.

Ain't nobody needs that!

Talk to your doctor. Talk to friends who are going through it or who went through it. But do yourself (and your sanity) a favor and don't turn to the internet.

Book your appointments at convenient times. If you need chemo or radiation, feel free to take your personal life into consideration. I planned to work during my treatments, so I booked my chemo treatments on Fridays so I had two days to recover before returning to work. Radiation either first thing in the morning on my way to work or over lunch, because it didn't take long. This is your life. Make it work for you.

Find a "Look Good, Feel Better" class and go. (www.lookgoodfeelbetter.org) Founded by the Personal Care Products Council Foundation and partnering with the American Cancer Society, The Look Good, Feel Better Foundation offers free classes locally that provide makeup instruction, scarf tying and other tips that will teach you use a variety of techniques to feel better about your appearance while going through cancer treatments. You may think you don't need to learn how to apply makeup, but trust me, you will be glad you attended! You will get lots of beauty tips—and some cool samples as well. Find a class online or contact your local chapter of the American Cancer Society to find a class.

Also before your first treatment, I suggest having these things on hand: stool softener; laxatives; anti-diarrhea medication; pantyliners; Replens; Preparation H; tissues; lip balm; Aquaphor, makeup concealer; eyeliner; eyebrow pencil; bathroom tissue. You will need most of those items.

1

Welcome to My Life

"If you can't say something nice ... smile politely and say 'fine.'"

If you're like me, you probably haven't paid much attention to breast cancer beyond periodic breast checks and maybe annual mammograms and, possibly, the purchase of the pink-lined Longaberger basket or Pampered Chef item from which a portion of the proceeds benefits a breast cancer cause.

Or maybe you have a friend or relative who had breast cancer and you followed her journey on social media (and always breathed a sigh of relief that it wasn't YOUR journey).

You probably never wanted to think about it or consider that you may one day have cancer.

That was me.

In fact, I was always rather annoyed every October when everything around me seems to not have turned the crisp yellow and gold colors of nature, but instead a pink hue, as if ribbons and shoelaces and postage stamps and even garage trucks have been visited by The Pink Panther in that classic episode, "The Pink Phink," where he paints everything pink.

As the editor of a parenting magazine at the time, I did the obligatory annual breast cancer issue because it's important to women and, frankly, because advertisers are more willing to spend their money on causes. We always interviewed survivors to give the message of hope. But I never read the issue beyond the proof-reading and editing requirements of the job.

Frankly, I didn't want to THINK about being a survivor, because that meant thinking of the alternative, and with a daughter at home, I just didn't want to go there.

So imagine my surprise when I was diagnosed with breast cancer at age 46.

Let me be honest: I never intended to write about it. But because I'm someone who has always faced life's challenges by journaling, I started making a few notes here and there about things that frustrated me.

And then I started thinking about writing a first-person story for our magazine—just to let other moms going through this that they aren't alone and because I now feel strongly that every woman needs a screening mammogram.

The more I wrote, the more I realized three things:

1. This really sucks.
2. There are so many women out there who have been through or are going through this.
3. I am really, really sarcastic. I guess it's a coping mechanism. I've never seen or heard anything about this disease that isn't sympathetic or hopeful. For someone like me, all that support literature they give you is a turn-off. How many sympathetic looks can one woman take?! How many, "Are you OKs?" can I answer before I scream, "No, I'm NOT OK, you moron!

It's never going to be OK again!" But yet, I managed my tone and smiled politely each time someone asked.

I finally decided that I can't be the only cynical patient. Surely, someone else out there has experienced what I'm going through but has no other vantage point besides the pleasant, sympathetic, victim approach. I didn't want pity. I just wanted to get through whatever I had to go through and be as normal as I could be.

(If you are the type of person who wants sympathy, there is nothing wrong with that. Enjoy it! That just wasn't me.)

So I offer to you, my experience, in hopes you will somehow find comfort in it—or at least amusement.

Please know that your journey will be different than mine. Your treatment may be different than mine. How you respond to treatment will probably be different. I don't mean to downplay or criticize anyone's diagnosis or how they respond to it. This book is for those who want to take their treatment in stride. It's also intended to be a conversation starter for those who are sharing the journey with a friend or family member.

No one knows what it's like to walk in your shoes. You may struggle to share details. This book may help you (or your friends and family) open up a dialogue so they know what questions to ask and may offer some basic understanding of what you are dealing with.

This is not medical advice. I am not a doctor or an expert. Talk with your physician for that.

Your takeaway: You are entitled to feel however you want about cancer and/or your own personal situation. You can be sad or angry or determined—whatever gets you through it! But don't forget to look for the joy and humor in things, too!

2

A Moment of Fright is No Delight

Jinkies! It looks like we've stumbled upon something suspicious!

Let me confess right here that I put off one mammogram. ONE! I had a good reason, I guess.

I always scheduled my mammograms immediately following my annual OB/GYN appointment because the offices were in the same building.

At this particular GYN appointment, they found "something suspicious" and sent me for an ultrasound.

My grandmother had died of ovarian cancer, so I was instantly full of anxiety. I remember lying on the table wondering if I was going to be diagnosed, too.

Fortunately, that wasn't my issue.

But because of that anxiety—and the fact that it was in the middle of a work day and I really had to get back to the office—I opted to forego the mammogram, with the promise of rescheduling it.

However, I didn't return for the mammogram. My bad!

A year later, when I walked into the radiology office for the now-overdue procedure, I wasn't nervous at all.

I never enjoy having my breasts smashed on the cold, hard metal, but my doctor has these pink spongy adhesives that cushion things a bit, so it's not terrible. And Myra, the mammography technician, has been doing my mammos for years and I enjoy catching up on what her children are doing.

It was a Tuesday in December when I walked in to visit with Myra.

The mammogram room where I go each year is rather spacious, but dimly lit. There is a machine in the middle of the room where I stand to have the pictures taken and a little machine in the corner where Myra views what she's doing.

She took several angles as usual and sent them off to have a radiologist review them.

Next thing I knew, the phone rang and Myra handed me the receiver.

You would think I'd have panicked at that point, but nope.

The young-sounding woman on the other end of the phone introduced herself as a doctor of radiology (whose name I didn't catch because it was just as foreign-sounding as my own) and said there was "something suspicious" on the mammogram.

Let me stop right here.

Growing up, I watched Scooby Doo and the gang. I read the Nancy Drew/Hardy Boys books. My favorite, by far, was a series called "The Three Investigators," so I was always intrigued, if not excited, when "something suspicious" came up. Perhaps that's why I wasn't worried.

The doctor explained that it *could be* a type of cancer, but she wasn't sure. She suggested a bioposy.

I remember asking her, "What if it IS cancer?"

She assured me that it was likely an early stage and that they could remove it with surgery.

Aside from the fact that I didn't want to go "under the knife," I wasn't worried at all.

It was just a few weeks before Christmas and I didn't want to think about my health over the holidays, so I opted to wait until January for the procedure.

After all, this was gonna be no big deal and I'd be enjoying Scooby snacks in no time!

Silly me.

During the holiday, I put the biopsy out of my mind.

But as the time got closer, I started to get worried. And so I did what many people today do—I turned to my peeps on social media.

"OK all you witty people...I am about to have my boob smashed for a half hour and have a large needle jabbed into it. Post something funny/interesting to distract me please. Thanks!!"

I did this not for sympathy. I have a lot of funny friends and I really wanted a distraction.

A while later, I got a private message from a friend who wanted to talk via phone. I called her. She told me she, too, has to go for a biopsy. She said, "I read your FB post about going for a biopsy and thought, 'who would write that?!' But I thought at least I know what she's going through."

We were both scared. She told me a story about a friend of hers who has a different kind of cancer and has a grim prognosis. "It could be worse," I thought.

Biopsies are traumatic experiences. I think it's because you don't know what you are dealing with, but you know it could be serious.

The fear of not knowing is tough!

It was a cold, gray, January afternoon when I went for my biopsy.

I asked my mother to drive, as I wasn't sure what to expect in terms of pain.

I was nervous. I knew they were going to shove a needle into my breast, but I wasn't exactly sure how they would do it.

As instructed, I slipped out of my sweater and bra and into a gown-like shirt that tied at the waist. I sat down in the waiting room and waited to be called back.

"Good luck, ladies," said a young woman as she walked past the waiting room on her way out the door.

I thought it odd. I didn't need luck … did I? … I wondered, as I flipped through the pages of an old "Better Homes & Gardens" magazine.

Before long, I was called to a small office where they had me fill out the typical paperwork prior to having any kind of procedure done.

One question the paperwork asked was how I wanted to receive my test results—by phone or in person?

I opted for the phone option, because I really didn't want to return and I figured everything would be OK.

Moments later, I was sitting in a dark room where the biopsy would take place. I remember tugging on the shirt a few times because it seemed it just wouldn't stay closed and, well, I didn't want my boobs hanging out!

Just as I had adjusted myself so that I was adequately covered, in walked a woman in a white lab coat and dark pants.

According to the blue embroidery, her name was Dr. Meredith Watts.

She had reddish-brown, wavy hair falling onto her shoulders and she was wearing comfortable-looking shoes. I believe you can tell a lot about a person by the shoes they are wearing, and I instantly determined she was practical, down-to-earth and smart, so I felt pretty confident in her presence.

She was holding a clipboard with my paperwork on it. She introduced herself and began asking me questions, as most doctors do when they first meet you—usually the same questions you just spent the last 10 minutes going over with the nurse.

And then she said, "I see you noted here that you'd prefer to get your results over the phone."

I told her that I did, indeed.

She asked if I was going to be out of town later in the week and couldn't return for my results.

She had a very serious look on her face, but I figured she just didn't have much of a bedside manner and probably had had a long morning.

So I repeated that I simply preferred to not have to come for another doctor visit.

She flinched as if she didn't care for my answer.

She seemed like a bottom-line kind of woman. I couldn't understand why we were wasting time going back and forth over this.

After a few more ping-pong rounds over this one, simple question that seemed to be a HUGE deal, I employed my sly, yet aggressive, journalist skills and demanded to know why I had to return in person.

"Because I'm pretty certain this will come back malignant," she finally said.

I think I stopped breathing.

I looked at her again, in that long, white lab coat, and waited for her to pull it and a mask off to reveal someone—anyone other than a doctor with bad news—because, well, that's generally what happens in the cartoon mysteries.

But there was no group of meddling kids and their dog in this episode.

There would be no trip to the malt shop.

Instead, I was directed to a light box on the wall where Dr. Watts (Ha! I just noticed the irony. Watts … light box …) who slapped my mammogram film up and pointed to a section on it. I looked and saw nothing.

Clearly, I needed more clues!

She moved her finger over a pattern that looked like tiny grains of sand. That, she said, is typical of a ductal carcinoma in situ breast cancer.

Tiny grains of sand. Really?! How could that be serious?!

I laid down on the table and Dr. Watts began the procedure. She numbed my breast (or so she thought) and then inserted a long needle into my breast. I couldn't see what was happening because I was facedown on a table, but I could feel it! She stopped and gave me more numbing agent.

Yes, I said "agent," because it was the secret agent that would make my boob numb!

Fortunately, the procedure didn't take too long, but as my breast became numb, I think I became emotionally numb, too.

This was no fun adventure. This was serious reality.

I don't remember getting dressed, but I remember walking out to the waiting room, seeing my mother sitting in a chair reading and feeling tears roll down my cheeks. "Let's go," I told her, as I kept walking towards the glass doors, through which I could see it had started to snow.

"That doesn't sound like good news," she said, as she picked up her coat and followed me.

By the time we reached the parking lot, I was full-on crying.

"They think it's cancer," I said, as I cradled a little round pillow they gave me underneath my left breast to protect it from being jostled in transit.

I thought back to the young woman who passed the waiting room. I guess I did need that "good luck" after all.

Your takeaway: It's really no mystery! If you're reading this and you don't have breast cancer, make sure you get a mammogram whenever you are eligible! Encourage your friends and family members to get their annual exams. Sure, it's uncomfortable and scary, but the earlier something is picked up, the more likely it is treatable, if not curable. If you have had breast cancer and still need mammograms, but are afraid, don't be. Do it. Then treat yourself to a Scooby snack of something tasty afterwards! You earned it!

3

Tissues, Tears and Tenderness

Here a boob, there a boob, everywhere a boob, boob.

The next thing I knew, my mother and I were back at the breast clinic getting the results of my biopsy. It was important to have someone with me, they warned.

I was single at the time, but seriously dating a man and, well, that's not the kind of thing you ask of a guy you've only known about seven months, so I invited my mom along again.

We walked into the waiting room and took a seat. I looked around and noticed women of all ages. I wondered if they were there for routine check-ups or something more serious.

My mother started reading her book as I sat and scrolled through Facebook, because I wanted to forget for a moment where I was.

After what seemed like an eternity, we were called back to a little board room with a round table in the middle.

The first thing I noticed was a tissue box on the center of the table. I glared at the tissue box—that can't be good, I thought—and sat down.

A patient advocate and the resident doctor followed me into the room.

Yes, indeed, it was cancer. An early stage, they thought. Stage 0, they thought. I would need an MRI and more tests to determine what type, and then I would have some decisions to make.

My mother took copious notes (I never fully appreciated her need for being detail-oriented until that day) as the doctor said which steps came next. I was glad she was there as back-up, although I had immediately gone into "reporter mode" as I was trained to do, which seemed to take the emotion out of what I was hearing.

Stage 0. Is that even serious? If it is Stage 0, is it really even cancer?

If you are reading this and thinking, "Well, it's just Stage 0 …" stop. Spoiler alert: It wasn't Stage 0.

You know, it really doesn't matter what stage of cancer it is. It's still cancer—in your body—that you have to get rid of.

My goal was simple: Understand what they were telling me.

I won't lie, it was difficult hearing the preliminary diagnosis and trying to understand everything the doctor was were telling me.

But for me, what made it more difficult was the tone being used and the expressions on the faces of the nurses and doctors. In most cases, it was a look of pity.

OK, so it probably wasn't pity. It was probably sympathy. But the look is the same. In just two medical tests, I had become a victim and I didn't much like that feeling.

At one point, I must have started to tear up because Nicole, the advocate, gently slid the tissue box across the table toward me. I grabbed a tissue, dabbed my eyes, and stuffed it up my sleeve, because that's what I tend to do with tissues since my second-grade teacher, Miss Mitzi Smith, taught me to do, rather than disturbing class to get up and throw them away.

In second grade, I didn't much care for the idea of having snot up my sleeve, but at this point, a slimy arm was the least of my worries.

When the doctor was done talking, we got up to leave. The resident put her hand on my shoulder and gave me a reassuring smile. Nicole gave me a hug.

Clearly, I had a supportive team in my corner!

Before I left the office, I received a kind pat on the hand and more sad eyes turned my way.

Maybe some people like that touchy-feely sympathetic stuff. I am not one of them.

It just made me feel sad. And I didn't want to feel sad. But something told me it was gonna be a while before I felt happy again.

I remember returning to work after the appointment. I told my boss and a couple of close friends.

And that is when everything in my world began to change.

There's an old expression, "it's all gone pear-shaped" that describes something that's taken a turn for the worse.

In my case, everything went boob-shaped.

I remember sitting at my desk, peeling a clementine. It looked good from the outside, but inside, it had a rotten spot. You never think about how much a peeled clementine looks and feels like a human breast until you've had a mammogram that shows all the little white veins and lines and calcifications. (OK, maybe for some of you, it's an orange, or if you're blessed with really big girls, a grapefruit, but for me and my aging, sagging breasts, it was more like a clementine.) I realized that clementine was like my boob—OK from the outside, but rotting from the inside.

I cried a bit and then ate around the bad part.

I quickly discovered I really couldn't escape my troubles. Apparently, I had checked my mental "happy place" at the door of the Women's Breast Center in Hershey, Pa.

From then on, every day when I opened my email, there was a Victoria's Secret offer featuring a deal on a new, sexy bra.

After the third email, I thought, 'Really?! I may no longer need a bra, let alone a sexy one!'

I cried a bit and then hit "UNSUBSCRIBE."

Then, I started noticing cleavage—in magazines, on celebrities on TV, on every woman I laid eyes on. I am certain I paid more attention to women's boobs than did my horny high school boyfriend!

Everyone I laid eyes on suddenly seemed to have a nice rack.

I cried a bit and then tried to stop looking at boobs.

If it wasn't breasts, it was cancer—on the radio in commercials, stories in magazines, interviews on TV. I couldn't escape the reality I was suddenly dealing with.

I cried a little every time I heard a TV commercial for Cancer Treatment Centers of America or read a magazine featuring a story about someone with cancer. And I'm telling you now, after you've been diagnosed, you realize nearly everyone must have some form of cancer!

Let me stop there for a second.

You may have noticed I cried a time or two.

Actually, I started crying a lot!

I cried every time I was reminded of boobs or cancer. I cried when I looked at my daughter. I cried when I went home after a date with my boyfriend.

And I wondered why the heck they can't make a mascara that resists copious amounts of tears but doesn't dry out your lashes!

But I tried to never cry in front of anyone. Because, well, big girls don't cry.

Your takeaway: Love your rack! Seriously. Who cares if your boobs are real or fake, small or saggy or so darned big they hurt your back?! Cherish them. Treat them well. They are yours for as long as you've got them. And it's OK to cry now and then. And remember, Kleenex says, "bless you."

4

Another Diagnostic Test of Strength

"My secrets to reveal ... for you are a magnet and I am steel."

—*"Magnet and Steel"* by Walter Egan

The next step for me was to get an MRI—Magnetic Resonance Imaging, in case you aren't familiar with the term.

I was to go to the office where they would give me an IV and put me into a machine that, they said, would be loud and confining.

They encouraged me to bring a CD to listen to, so I happily made a mix CD of tunes that made me feel happy.

I decided to go to this appointment alone, because it wasn't far from my office and it was in the middle of the day.

I crammed the CD into my purse and went to the office where they were to do the procedure.

I was instructed to disrobe and change into a gown and socks and let my clothes and belongings in a locker.

I did as instructed, grabbed my CD and headed into the room.

This was the appointment I dreaded.

I was so afraid I was actually shaking as I walked into a very cold room with a very large machine in the middle.

I took a seat where the nurse took my arm to look for a vein for the IV.

I warned her this wasn't likely to be an easy task and we both chuckled nervously about that.

Again, I shook, I'm not sure if it was from being nervous or from the temperature of the room. As she went to fetch me a warm blanket, I sat there wondering: This is a giant, magnetic machine, will metal come ripping out of my body? Did I swallow a penny as a child?! Oh, please tell me they didn't leave any clips or things inside me when I had my C-section 20-some years ago!

I mentioned my concerns to the nurse who assured me I would be just fine!

The IV successfully in, I was placed on the machine.

They warned me about the noise, and it was loud and sounded like it does when you sit at the rear of a commuter plane—kind of a tinny, steady hum.

I was placed face down and told dye would be injected into my IV. They handed me headphones and an emergency button to hit in case I needed a break or something.

As the dye coursed thru my veins, I could feel it move through my arms, chest, feet. It made me feel anxious. What if it caused a heart attack? What if I died right there and couldn't push the emergency button?

The calming mix of '70s tunes I had copied to the CD were barely audible and did little to distract me from the machine that hummed, clicked and banged around me.

Just about the time I got used to the noises and found some comfort in the music, it was over and I was removed from the tube and told they would send the results to my doctor and I should wait for a phone call in a day or two.

Again, the nurses and attendants were very sympathetic to my plight. Even the receptionist gave me the "pity smile" as I checked out.

"STOP BEING NICE," I thought. "You all are freaking me out!"

Still shaking, I opened the door to the waiting room. There, sitting in a chair opposite the door, was a graphic designer I worked with. She was expecting a baby at the time and I assume was there for an ultrasound.

Once again, fate stepped in and just seeing a familiar face took away my nerves.

I headed back to work thinking the worst was over.

Silly me. The worst hadn't even begun.

A day or so later, at work, I got a call. The MRI showed something "suspicious" (I really began to hate that term!). I would need an ultrasound—of both breasts.

I immediately went upstairs and cried in my boss's office.

I know that's unprofessional, but I couldn't control myself.

He gave me a hug and a tissue and talked to me until I could pull myself together.

I returned to my office where I had a baggie of grapes, which I thought I'd snack on.

The first two tasted like 100 percent insecticide. I look at the bag and wondered if I should pitch them all.

Then I asked myself, "In the grand scheme of things, is this is a big deal? Will eating a chemically-ridden grape cause me to die today?" I decided "no" and ate them all.

Yippee for the cancer diagnosis! It makes you realize something really *could* kill you, but odds are it's not gonna be a few bad grapes.

At this point in the process, I realized my life (and sanity and sense of "normal") was hanging in the balance of the next test and test result.

When you begin this journey, the tests never seem to end!

From a mammogram to another mammogram to a biopsy to an MRI to an ultrasound … you'd better get used to doctors' offices, and hopefully, if you work, you have personal time you can take to go to the appointments.

I was very fortunate. I had a boss who understood. I worked for a company that had a fabulous paid time off program that allowed up to three hours for every doctor appointment without having to use personal leave. I appreciated that prior to this diagnosis, but afterwards, that became an invaluable benefit.

I worked in a supportive environment. I had great support at home. I was strong as steel! I'd get through this!

Your takeaway: Go ahead. Make a mix CD! Call it your mojo music or make one for a friend. Also, eat the grapes! Or the cake. Or the doughnut. Everything in moderation. You are strong! You are steel!

: 5

Seeking Focus and Finding Faith

"Never be lonely lost in the night, just run from the darkness, looking for the light. 'Cause it's a long hard road that leads to a brighter day, don't let your heart grow cold, just reach out and call His name, His name."

—"Yah Mo Be There" by James Ingram and Michael McDonald

One thing you never think about when you think of someone going through something like this (or at least I never did) is what it does to your mind.

Some people get depressed. Some people feel sorry for themselves. Some people go into fight mode and find a determination they didn't know they had.

For me, it was an introduction to major anxiety.

I didn't tell too many people about what was going on. I didn't want pity, but I also didn't want to be reminded of my plight.

As hard as I tried to not think about it between tests, I found when I wasn't focused on work or on a task, fear crept up on me.

I began to structure my time to ensure that I had little mental down time and little alone time.

At night, as I crawled into bed, I would watch HGTV or "Storage Wars" or taped episodes of "The Bold and the Beautiful" to take my mind off my troubles until I was exhausted and fell asleep.

Once I slept, I usually slept soundly.

But there were the occasional reminders.

Even HGTV had the occasional commercial for a cancer treatment drug. I picked up a copy of "People" magazine, expecting fluffy entertainment news, only to page through to a story about a young woman with cancer.

"God, this is depressing! I can't escape it," I thought.

And then there were the becoming-more-frequent chats and phone calls from well-intended friends and family.

"Just calling to see how you made out with your test" and "How are you feeling?"

Well, gee, I was feeling great until you called and now I have to think about how I'm feeling and I'm feeling like this sucks.

And then there are those super thoughtful people who feel compelled to show their empathy by telling you stories about their grandmother, aunt, cousin, etc., who died of the disease.

Um, yeah, thanks, I really didn't need to hear that! I'm frightened enough, thanks.

But, bless their hearts, they meant well, I guess.

One day, however, I woke up and just wanted to punch someone in the face.

I was angry. Can't these people just stop being worried?! Can't they stop looking at me with pity?! Can't we all just go about our lives and forget this is happening?!

I looked at the calendar. I had two days before I had to go for the ultrasound.

And so I vowed that for the next two days, I would forget this was happening.

Henceforth, I was going to live day by day!

And that's when I realized something really important. I had never lived day by day before.

I was the type of person who was always looking towards the future.

When I was a kid, I had little in common with kids may age, so I couldn't wait to grow up.

As a young adult, I looked forward to getting married ... and starting a family ... and buying a home ... and buying a bigger home ... and so on.

I was all about the destination. I had zero patience for the journey.

My journey had changed prior to my diagnosis. I got divorced after 20 years of marriage. My only child went off to college. I found myself alone for the first time.

I never considered myself a religious person, but I was always spiritual.

I prayed every night, as if God was Santa and I offered up my wish list of things I wanted for Christmas. I asked God for everything from patience, to good friends, to healthy family relationships, to thicker hair and perkier boobs!

I asked Him to fix what was wrong with me that prevented me from having a healthy, loving relationship.

I wanted less anger and more patience. I wanted to find happiness. I wanted to appreciate what I had.

Suddenly, in one moment, I realized I had to have patience. I had to be focused on living day by day, because there was absolutely no way of knowing what was gonna come at me next.

"Well," I remember thinking, "I guess God has given me patience."

I had no idea at that time that His gifts were gonna keep on giving.

Your takeaway: Have faith. Whatever that faith is, have faith in something. Find an outlet for expressing that faith, whether it's prayer or a walk in the woods, but practice it each and every day. You'll be amazed by what happens.

6

Test Anxiety

*"I got a disease, deep inside me, makes me feel uneasy baby
… Keep your distance from it
Don't pay no attention to me. I got a disease."*

—"Disease" by Matchbox Twenty

I mentioned my anxiety. It got so bad that I couldn't cross the threshold of a doctor's office without my blood pressure and heart rate skyrocketing off the charts.

The nurses started taking my blood pressure and pulse twice each visit because they were concerned.

This boggled my mind! I mean, I've always thought I was pretty good at controlling myself and my emotions. I thought I was good at relaxing. But nothing I tried worked to bring those numbers down.

I was offered a mild sedative that I could take before each appointment to take the edge off. I hate taking medication, but I did take it once or twice before appointments because I decided it was better to pop an Ativan than to have a heart attack or stroke because I couldn't control my anxiety.

I returned to the Breast Center for the ultrasound of my boobs—both of them, as the MRI showed several questionable areas in both of them.

I walked into another dark room where I was directed to lay on the table by a resident named Dennis, a radiology resident, who was more worried about my modesty than I was at that point, as he gently made sure I was covered on the opposite side from where they removed another crappy hospital wrap. Was he even serious? I mean, this dude looks at boobs all day. And I have always been an extremely self-conscious and modest person, but by this point, my girls had become less something I associated with a sexy body and more something I associated with science, so flashing them was becoming something that didn't bother me much at all.

As for the ultrasound procedure, you ladies who had a maternity ultrasound know that they take a wand and run it over your skin, allowing them to see a picture of what's inside. That is how this was over my breasts.

The room was cold again, or maybe I was just nervous. The radiologist, Alison Chetlen, was super friendly. She recognized my name from my job as a local magazine editor and we chatted about kids and families and parenting as she did the procedure.

I admire her and Dennis because neither looked at me with those darned sad eyes. They both talked as if we were just friends chatting about stuff. I felt almost human!

She opted to take another biopsy, this time with something that reminded me of an Epipen and it didn't hurt much at all.

Before I knew it, it was over and I could feel my pulse returning to normal as I got dressed.

Maybe for a while, at least, my life could go back to normal (whatever that is now) until the results come back.

Your takeaway: You can't control everything and life is scary sometimes. It will be OK! But you don't have to shake in silence. Ask for help. It's OK to need help.

7

Life

"That's life (that's life) that's what people say. You're riding high in April, shot down in May.
But I know I'm gonna change that tune when I'm back on top, back on top in June."

—*"That's Life" by Frank Sinatra*

At this point, I had the mammogram, biopsy, MRI, ultrasound and additional biopsy. It had been less than a month since my diagnosis and I'd been to more doctors' offices in a few weeks than I had been in my adult life.

I had been poked and prodded and felt-up more times than I could imagine—and the last not in a the way that makes you feel all tingly!

It sucked, but that's life.

You know, when I was in fifth grade, there was a silly saying going around that you said with your friends. It went like this:

Me: That's life!
Friend: What's life?
Me: A magazine.

Friend: How much does it cost?
Me: 50 cents.
Friend: I only have 25.
Me: Well, that's life!
(and then we'd repeat it until we got bored or someone told us to shut up.)

I still grin when I recite that little ditty. But it's so true. It is what it is. There are some things you can't change and you never have enough.

It's just life and life goes on … you hope.

And in between tests, my life did go on.

I tried to stick to my routine and be as "normal" as I could. And I relied on the people around me to help me with that.

I will get into more on this later, but at this point, I wasn't sure exactly what I was dealing with. All I knew was I had an early stage of breast cancer and was facing some kind of treatment which would definitely involve surgery and radiation.

That's the thing about this disease. There are so many types and stages and everyone has a different kind and stage. There is no one treatment.

I had to decide if I wanted a lumpectomy or a mastectomy, meaning did I want them to remove the cancerous tissue or did I want them to remove the entire breast?

I talked at length with my doctors and weighed all the information and statistics.

My grandmother had died with ovarian cancer, so there was a chance I had the BRCA gene.

BRCA1 and BRCA2 are human genes that produce tumor suppressor proteins. When the gene is mutated, the proteins aren't produced or don't function as they should and cells are more likely to develop additional genetic alterations that can lead to cancer.

Some of these inherited gene mutations increase the risk of breast and ovarian cancer.

There is a test to determine if you have these genes. It's not a cheap test and insurance doesn't always cover it, but I opted for the test, figuring if I had the gene, I'd go for a mastectomy.

If I did not, I would go for the lumpectomy, since in my case, the end results of treatment were projected about the same.

Of course, it takes multiple tests and multiple stages to figure out exactly what you are dealing with.

It takes time and patience.

I know my doctors did all they could to get me those answers quickly.

In fact, they wanted to move more quickly than I was ready for at times.

I preferred to accept my information in small, spaced apart increments. I didn't want to be overwhelmed. And it can be VERY overwhelming.

But I managed my appointments and my schedule. I didn't drop everything for the next appointment just because that was the first available date on the doctor's calendar.

I figured out early on that this journey wasn't going to be a few days or weeks or a few months, but I had no idea how long it would take. I hoped it would be short and sweet, but I had no plan yet. I just had to roll with what I knew day by day, week by week.

And, by golly, I was not gonna let the pesky doctor appointments and tests throw off my routine!

And so every day, I got up and went to work. And every day, I went home, ate supper and watched TV and went about my normal activities like I always did and like most normal people do.

I hung out with friends and family and lived my life until the next interruption.

And on the days when I was down, I knew I'd be back up the next day. Because that's life!

Your takeaway: You will have ups and downs. You may not always have the time and energy for what's in front of you. But that's life! Don't let it wear you down. Tomorrow is another day and you'll win that one for sure!

8

Getting Answers

> *"I don't want to know the reasons why love keeps right on walking on down the line. I don't want to stand between you and love, honey, I just want you to feel fine."*
>
> —"I Don't Want To Know" by Fleetwood Mac

There are some things you don't really want to know.

As much as I needed to know what I was dealing with and what would come next, I really didn't *want* to know.

I just wanted it to go away. I wanted to be OK.

I mean, I *felt* fine! Surely, this couldn't be THAT big of a deal, right?

After each test, I breathed a sigh of relief having gotten through it, but dreaded the call with results.

Would the cancer be limited to my left breast or would it be in both? What about my lymph nodes?

Would surgery take care of this or would I need radiation? (At this point, chemotherapy wasn't even on my radar.)

I hoped at some point, maybe I'd get over my heart racing every time the phone rang, every time they wanted a new test. But I wasn't there yet.

It was coming up on Valentine's Day—a time when everything turns red and pink. Pink was always my favorite color and the brighter, the better. My childhood bedroom was a nice Pepto-Bismol hue. But I was coming to hate the color since it represents breast cancer.

I had been Catholic for a time in my life, so I started attending Mass.

The parish where I was attending announced a Feast of St. Blasé blessing where the priest would perform an anointing of the throat, which includes the head, neck and covers anything you might speak as well. So I attended and got my blessing, because it couldn't hurt, right?!

While there, I decided I needed every player in the game, so I booked a Catholic penance because it had been years since I participated fully in the Catholic Church and I wanted to do things the right way.

I left both feeling empowered. I mean, like TV evangelist Joyce Meyer says, if God was for me, who could be against me?

I lived in my happy bubble of faith and protection for a couple days before I got what I knew was coming: the dreaded ultrasound, biopsy and BRCA results.

The call came when I was in a meeting at work and I had left my phone on my desk. I returned to find a voicemail from the nurse asking me to return her call at my earliest convenience.

Of course panic ensued, because if everything was OK, wouldn't she just have said everything was OK when she left the message?

I immediately went into full anxiety mode with my heart racing. I began shaking.

Thank God for a colleague and friend, Hope, whose office was next to mine at the time. I grabbed my phone and went into her office and asked her if I could sit with her as I made the call because I feared bad news. She graciously stopped what she was doing and watched and waited as I made the call. Now, I guess I had God and Hope alongside me, so I was well armed.

The nurse answered. Everything was OK with the other breast, she said. The lymph nodes looked clear. I was BRCA negative, so we would proceed with surgery on the left breast.

Of course, I'd need some bloodwork and an EKG before surgery, but otherwise, no new tests.

What a relief!

You may or may not believe in the power of prayer. You may consider it the power of positivity or the power of hope. That's OK. But I believe. And I was pretty darned grateful.

One step closer to this journey being complete!

Your takeaway: The stress of waiting for test results can be taxing. You can either want them instantly or never want them. But it's better to know what you are dealing with so you can begin to fix it. It's also good to have a friend either along for the ride or on the sidelines cheering. Don't be afraid to ask for support when you need it!

9

Off the Pill and Off the Rails

"Mental wounds still screaming, driving me insane. I'm goin' off the rails on a crazy train. I'm goin' off the rails on a crazy train"

—"Crazy Train" by Ozzy Osbourne

I was determined to have a great week. There were no tests, no results to come back and no dreaded phone calls anticipated.

I spent two days at work returning to a happy normal.

I followed social media as usual, only to discover a high school classmate had passed away. I scrolled through the comments and searched for the obituary like a mad woman, looking to see what caused his demise. Was it cancer?! Ohmygosh, if he died, I could die!

As it turns out, he passed peacefully (yet way too early) in his sleep and it wasn't related to cancer.

OK, so death can happen to any of us. I shouldn't panic about cancer killing me. I could just as easily get hit by a bus while crossing the street.

Crisis averted, I resumed my routine. As editor of a monthly parenting magazine, it was my job to proofread and edit all the content in the publication.

I had a freelance writer who submitted monthly columns about relationships. I always looked forward to his articles because they were usually pretty upbeat and honest.

I open the email. This one, of course, happened to be all about handling death and dying.

Really?! Can't I just get away from all this?!

Let me be honest … (And if you are a guy reading this, just stop now and page through to the next chapter, please, unless you are reading this because you have a wife, mother, daughter or woman friend who you are supporting in her journey. Then, by all means, read on.)

As if a cancer diagnosis wasn't traumatic enough, mine happened to be an estrogen-sensitive type, meaning estrogen can feed its growth.

I had been on the birth control pill for most of my life, mainly because I always had an irregular cycle.

The doctors highly recommended stopping the pill so as not to throw hormones at the cancer.

So here I was with an unpredictable cycle.

And here I was at work, discovering said cycle can begin at any time of the month and can be quite heavy.

"OMG, this is horrid! How do women DO this every month," I wondered.

Seriously, not only had Aunt Flow suddenly come to visit, she clearly brought her kids and her friends and her dog!

Since the Pennsylvania Emergency Management Agency had not issued a flood warning for my nether region, I was totally unprepared for a crisis of this magnitude.

I dropped what I was doing (the column on death and dying was going to have to wait at least until I determined I was not, in fact, dying) and walked to my nearest colleague of child-bearing age to inquire as to whether she had any feminine hygiene products I could have.

Fortunately, her desk drawer was better stocked than mine and I took care of the immediate need.

But was this normal? I was in my 40s and couldn't imagine this being normal.

I then did what anyone with an unusual malady would do, I got on Google.

One of the first "hits" that came up was Toxic Shock Syndrome.

I remembered hearing about that in my teen years. It comes from tampons, if I'm not mistaken.

OMG! What if I die from TSS?!

What if the cancer doesn't kill me but the TSS does? Wouldn't that be ironic?!

#hypochondriacmuch?

Heart racing, I picked up the phone and dialed my colleague who had saved the day. She picked up on the first ring.

"Hey, can you please come over," I whispered.

She returned a few minutes later.

"Shut the door," I instructed.

She did.

"So I know this is crazy, but should I be worried about toxic shock syndrome," I asked.

She looked at me and laughed. "No. I think you are fine," she said.

"Are you sure, because this can't be normal and what if I get TSS," I asked.

She walked around behind my desk, held her arms out and said, "Come here."

I stood up and she hugged me.

"You are fine," she said. "You are going to be fine. Just relax."

"But … ," I began.

"Seriously, you have nothing to worry about," she said. "And stop Googling."

I took a breath. She was right. I was being ridiculous.

But suddenly, every pain, itch and twitch seemed like bad news.

I had to stop worrying. I was going to be fine. Sometime. I hoped.

Your takeaway: Many things in your life may change due to your diagnosis. There's so much more to this than anyone tells you. Take it one thing at a time and, for the love of Ozzy, don't turn to the internet to diagnose your problems!

10

Music to My Ears

"Everybody's got a water buffalo.
Yours is fast but mine is slow.
Oh, where we'd get them, I don't know,
but everybody's got a water buffalo."

—"The Water Buffalo Song" by Veggie Tales

As my surgery date inched closer, I focused on having fun with my family.

My daughter and I had planned to attend a Fleetwood Mac Concert in Charlottesville, Va. We are both big fans of the group and try to attend their concerts whenever they are within driving distance. This was a big event for her and I didn't want to miss it, so I actually scheduled my surgery later than planned so I could attend the show.

Not only would it give me quality time with my daughter, it would help take my mind off my troubles.

Brooke and I hadn't really talked much about my diagnosis. I didn't want to frighten her and, frankly, didn't want to think about what would happen if the worst were to occur.

I knew she was scared, but all she really asked when I told her was, "You're going to be OK, right?"

And I had assured her that I would be fine.

As we headed south, she behind the wheel and I in the passenger seat, we discussed someone we both knew who was back at Johns Hopkins Medicine with a diagnosis of a very serious auto-immune disease. This woman and I were the same age.

"She's not doing well," Brooke said.

My stepfather, Terry Quinn, always said if we all took our problems into a room and dropped them onto a table and looked over everyone else's problems, odds are we'd choose to leave the room with our own, rather than trading for someone else's.

I thought about that in this scenario.

"You know, if I had to pick, I'd choose my disease over hers," I said. "But it seems like everyone's got something now. It reminds me of that old water buffalo song."

Quick-witted as ever, Brooke began singing her version of the Veggie Tales classic tune, "Everyone's got a water buffalo. Yours is deadly, mine grows slow."

Morbid? Yes. But it made us laugh! (Side note, our friend is doing much better!)

We didn't talk again about cancer or sickness, and we had a great time at the concert that night as we sang along to songs that went, "thunder only happens when it's raining" and "don't stop thinking about tomorrow."

I'm a big believer of music therapy and that, for me, was the best medicine ever!

Your takeaway: We all have a water buffalo. Don't let yours get you down. Let the music play! Sing! Have fun. Make memories.

And remember: "If you wake up and don't want to smile, if it take just a little while, open your eyes and look at the day, you'll see things in a different way!"

11

Sentinel Nodes and Surgery Day

A tale of red carpet, chocolate and wet wipes.

You don't think about all the marvels of modern medicine until you have to have some bizarre test.

I first thought about this when I was told I'd need a sentinel node biopsy to determine which lymph nodes my breast drained.

According to my surgeon, they inject a radioactive tracer and/or blue dye into the breast and the tracers then go to the first draining lymph node of the breast. The idea, she said, is if a cancer is going to spread, it is most likely going to spread to those lymph nodes first.

That way, during surgery, they can remove those lymph nodes to test them to see if there are cancer cells, she explained.

The procedure, surprisingly, was painless and simple for me.

Next up was surgery day.

Forty-eight hours before surgery, I still had no idea what I needed to do to prepare.

Should I eat? Not eat? How long would it take? How long would I be laid up?

This was never really explained when it was scheduled. All I got was the promise of getting details closer to the time.

I called the surgeon's office and was assured someone would call me the day before surgery. Seriously?! I finally work up the nerve to call them after admitting that yes, this really IS happening, and they put me off?

Where was all that touchy-feely, happy-to-help-you bullcrap they dumped on me before?

I just had a few simple questions. It couldn't possibly be that difficult! I mean, surely they knew the process and surely the operating room had been booked at that point. Couldn't they just take a minute and help me?

Nope.

I was clearly on my own.

Of all the things about this diagnosis that frightened me, the worst, by far, was the thought of surgery.

The only time I had had surgery in the past was an emergency C-section when I had my daughter 20 years ago and I was awake then, thanks to an epidural.

This time, I would be put out. What if I woke up during the procedure? What if the anesthesia didn't do its job? Or worse, what if I didn't come out from being under?

Imagine that! The cancer didn't kill me, but the surgery did. How awful would that be?

The next day, I got the calling giving me the particulars of the surgery and instructions for what to eat (nothing after midnight – I felt like a Gremlin).

It was an itinerary that rivaled any AAA trip plan I ever had.

I was to show up first at the Breast Center's radiology department, where they would insert wires into my breast so the surgeon knew exactly where to cut. We would then travel down the road to the hospital. A nurse would ride with me. We would have free valet parking when we got to the hospital. The surgery would be done and I could go home that day, assuming I came out of anesthesia OK.

Didn't that sound like a delightful day? Valet parking! Everything is classier with valet parking. I wondered if there would be a red carpet to follow and paparazzi, too.

The next day, my mother and I headed to Hershey at O-dark-hundred for surgery.

We started, as instructed, at the Breast Center, where I changed into the classic hospital wrap by a designer you've never heard of, accented it with a white, waffle-knit robe with "Penn State Breast Center" embroidered in pink, and waited to be escorted to a doctor's office answer to a green room where the pre-show would begin.

I was called to go into another dark, cold room, where my old buddy, Modest Dennis, the radiology resident waited for me.

You'd be surprised how a familiar face can have a calming effect, even when you are anticipating wires being shoved into your boob.

He explained the process and began the preparation, again, concerned about keeping me covered.

"Oh, please, Dennis," I said. "I'm not worried about modesty. You've seen my boobs more than my ex-husband of 20 years. Just let them hang out."

Dennis, who I am sure had seen so much in his developing career, had clearly never heard anything like that before. In the dim lighting, I could still notice his face turning a few shades of red. But hey, it lightened the mood as I was being poked and prodded.

It really wasn't that bad and it didn't take long at all.

As he was finishing up the insertion of the wires, in walked Dr. Watts. Of course! The stern woman who dropped the "M" bomb on me had returned for this episode of "The Woman & The Cancer."

I kept my head down, hoping she would review my film and I could exit stage left.

But then, it was as if someone whispered to me to reconsider. I decided I needed to get rid of the negative energy I had towards her. I mean, it wasn't her fault I was malignant. It wasn't (entirely) her fault I pushed her to disclose bad news.

I called her over. I wasn't sure she would remember me, because she has so many patients.

"Dr. Watts, you probably don't remember the day, but I was initially shocked and appalled when you told me you expected my biopsy to be malignant. But I am a bottom line person and you gave me the bottom line. Had you not been so forth-coming with me that day, I'd have suffered much more down the road. So I just want to thank you."

She looked at me and I saw her tough exterior soften just a bit.

"I do remember that day," she admitted. "I didn't want to tell you like that," she said.

We talked briefly about that day. We are both tough women, yet I think that day was traumatic for both of us.

I know I felt better when we finished chatting. I hope she did, too.

I felt grateful to have had the opportunity to have that conversation with her.

I was put back in the wrap and robe (which had to be ever-so-gently placed across my chest to cover the wires sticking out of my left breast) and assisted into my mother's car for the short drive to the hospital.

When we arrived, the valet was there to take the keys. There was no red carpet, no paparazzi, just the blackness that enveloped the front of Penn State Health Hershey Medical Center at the butt-crack of dawn.

I looked around and sniffed the air, because yes, often, it really does smell like chocolate in Chocolatetown. Of course, having had nothing to eat, this was one of those days when I could smell not only chocolate, but the fragrance of roasted peanuts from the Reese's factory. If only I could enjoy a Reese's Cup right now!

I thought about how the last time I was at the hospital for surgery under the cover of darkness, it had been when I delivered my daughter.

That was such a happy time!

And here I was, about to have something else removed from my body, but this time, I sure didn't want to take any parts of it home.

Funny how things change.

At the hospital, I was instructed to change and then take these large wet-wipe type things and wipe down in a very specific way. There was a chart on the wall to direct me in how many wipes to use per body part and which way to wipe.

They made it seem like this was a very critical step to the process and must be followed precisely.

Were they even serious?

I couldn't be responsible for this! Heck, when my daughter was a toddler and often had sticky hands and face, even SHE knew how poorly I was at being thorough. I usually did my best and then just handed her the wipe because I knew my job wasn't going to suffice for a picky 2-year-old and here I was, expected to kill every germ on my person with a very precise series of swipes.

As if I wasn't already worried about dying, now I had to worry that I would cause my own MRSA infection due to poor wiping.

Again, I was certain the breast cancer wouldn't kill me, the MRSA would!

I looked at my mother, who clearly was having flashbacks of finding dust and crumbs on every household surface I helped clean as a teenager, because she reached out her hand and said, "Here, let me help."

Once again, my mommy saved the day to ensure the baby she brought into the world wouldn't be taken out by a MRSA infection.

I then unwrapped a pack of yellow socks with treads on them—just like the orange ones they give you at the local indoor trampoline park—and slipped them on my feet. I actually slipped them over my own socks because even though they came in a sealed pack, I didn't want them next to my skin. I have no idea what that was about. It wasn't like they were rented bowling shoes, nor did I have a particular attachment to the socks I wore to the hospital, but that's what I did. I write it off to nerves.

While we waited, a steady stream of nurses came in to ask questions and take vital signs. They were all new faces, but very friendly.

We waited. And waited.

I got an IV and waited some more.

Finally, my surgeon, Dr. Kristine Widders, appeared from behind the curtain like an angel. (I swear to you, there was a glow around her!)

She's younger than I am, but has always exuded a quiet confidence and I like her.

She assured me we were next in line for the operating room and she was ready.

A nurse and a member of the transport team came to wheel me away and I was reminded to remove my glasses, which I handed to my mother when we reached the portion of the hallway where she would take the elevator to the waiting room and I would head to the OR.

At this point, it was me and the medical team, and one of us was legally blind without vision correction.

But maybe it was better that I couldn't see clearly.

We reached the OR and I was asked to slide from my bed with wheels to the operating table. After that, I saw my surgeon angel again and next thing I knew, I was waking up in a different room, my mother waiting at my side.

I was about two inches of tissue short of a boob and three less lymph nodes, but otherwise none the worse for the wear.

It was over! I made it! I got this!

Your takeaway: Just go with it. Do what you are told to the best of your ability. Rely on the professionals to do what they do best. And sometimes, just stop and smell the chocolate.

12

Surgery day: Take Two

"If at first you don't succeed ... you're running about average."

My biggest fear conquered, I was beginning to feel normal again. My breast felt swollen and achy, but nothing like I expected.

Frankly, the worst part was changing the dressing on it, as apparently, my skin is extremely sensitive to adhesives. (Funny how they always ask about latex allergies, yet no one mentioned adhesive troubles. I guess I'm a unicorn.)

I had a work trip planned to Baltimore the week after my surgery that included an awards ceremony and I wasn't about to miss it.

I took my healing, but still sore, boob and wireless bra and headed south where I was careful not to walk too quickly and not to sling my purse strap across my chest.

I had a lovely time at the convention, met some good friends and assumed I was well on my way to recovery.

By the time I returned to my regular work schedule, they called with the pathology report.

The bad news: It was an invasive type of cancer.

More bad news: My surgeon felt she didn't get enough of the margins, so she wanted to go back in and remove some more tissue.

No worries, Dr. Widders assured me, "We'll just go back in through the original incision."

Oh, goodie! Just about the time it's healed and no longer painful, they'll rip it open again. Yay!

At what point are my worst fears NOT going to be realized? That's what wanted to know.

When would this nightmare be over?

I just wanted things to go back to the old normal.

I scheduled the next surgery. At least I knew what to expect now. And, honestly, I didn't mind the second surgery. I'd much rather be safe than sorry later.

Because I knew exactly what to expect this time, I went into the second surgery with little fear and came through it well.

This second go-round was different, maybe because I was first surgery of the day. They got me in early for an 8 a.m. schedule.

"We'll send it out to make sure we got it all," Dr. Widders told me just before they wheeled me toward the OR.

Was she kidding?! There was a chance we'd have to go for a THIRD time?!

This time, I had a different anesthesiologist who I had little confidence in because she was trying so hard to please me.

I merely suggested that she put the IV in my wrist, rather than back of my hand because that's where it landed best the last time and she literally tripped over her own two feet trying to shove that baby into my wrist.

But to her credit (and mine, I guess) it worked.

Next, she said she was going to give me something to "relax" me prior to being wheeled into OR, but I mentioned that last time, all they said was "I'm going to give you something to relax you now" when I was actually IN the OR and I was out like a light.

Hearing that advice, she decided to wait.

It was a good thing I spoke up and a good thing she obeyed because there was a minor paperwork mix-up that had to be sorted out in the OR and that couldn't have been completed had I slipped under.

That fixed, they gave me something to relax me and I was out!

I had an easier time waking up, but a sore throat. Otherwise, I really felt better after surgery than I did before.

My breast felt better after the second surgery than it did before surgery which, my surgeon says, is because I had a large hematoma (bad bruise) inside my breast after the first surgery. During the second surgery, she drained the bruise, making me more comfortable.

Afterwards, I had less swelling and pain in my breast.

Now all I had to do was wait to meet with the oncologist to get my treatment plan. It was the first day of spring. It was snowing, but at least warm weather was on the way!

I was told I would need radiation.

Any additional treatment was to be determined by pathology reports on the tissue removed from my breast. I would have to wait for the results.

Some people don't like waiting for test results. I, on the other hand, preferred a few days of respite from bad news.

I knew I had at least a couple days before I had to think about cancer again. I enjoyed those days very much.

Your takeaway: You will have lots of tests during your journey. Sometimes, you'll get good results. Sometimes, you'll get news that's hard to take. Despite the bill of goods we were sold through all those darned Disney movies, things don't always go your way in the end. You just have to take it one day, one test at a time. Consider it a victory that you made it this far. Hope and pray for the best outcome. I believe having a positive outlook helps. I also believe in the power of prayer. Keep hoping and praying!

13

Keeping Chapter 13 at Bay

"Health is like money. We never have an idea of its true value until we lose it."

—*Anonymous*

The American Cancer Society called. A nice-sounding woman asked me how they could help. She suggested financial help with medical bills or maybe a support group.

Yes, my medical bills were piling up like snow in Boston during the winter of 2014, but I could only imagine the paperwork I'd need to fill out to get financial help.

And support groups? OMG. The last thing I wanted to do was sit in a room full of people talking about their cancer. Just shoot me, stat!

Let me just say it's bad enough to have cancer, but once you adjust to that diagnosis, then what is even more devastating, in a way, is how to pay for your illness.

This is true, I'm told, whether you have insurance or not.

I was very fortunate that I had good insurance through my job.

Within the first month of my diagnosis, I got hit with bills exceeding $2,000. By month two, that had doubled to more than $4,000—which was my health insurance deductible.

"Great," I thought. "My deductible will kick in and we'll be good."

What I didn't figure was how to pay for that first $4,000.

Fortunately, my hospital offered convenient payment plans. When I first called (at the $2,000 balance) the payment was an affordable $130.

But as more bills came in, the monthly tab went up to $350.

The $130 was manageable in my budget, thanks to a recent pay raise. The $350 was not.

They offered financial aid.

I initially turned it down because, well, I didn't want to fill out all their prying paperwork, plus, I didn't need financial aid. I was a working woman!

Silly me, I actually did need help.

As the bills piled up, I realized there was no way I was going to be able to pay off this ever-growing debt.

Some people I know in my situation turned to crowd-funding through social media. That wasn't something I was comfortable with.

I accepted the financial aid through my hospital, which made my tab manageable.

I'd like to say it got easier. But I've finished this book and, well, it doesn't.

Your takeaway: Take advantage of offers to help. Ask your doctor or hospital or healthcare facility if they have payment plans. Ask about financial aid and scholarships. Most larger hospitals have some benefits. Talk to the American Cancer Society, the Pa. Breast Cancer Coalition (or one like it in your state) and any other cancer organization for help. You can be proud or you can be poor!

14

> "Have you had any changes in your general health history?"

"Stupid is as stupid does."

– *Forrest Gump*

Another day, another medical appointment. This time, it was a regular dental check-up.

Of course, they ask about medications you are on and any change in health history. I said "no" because I really didn't need to see the look of pity on the young hygienist's face and then have to explain it all.

Unfortunately, it was time for dental X-rays. I declined (No! I said, a little too harshly.) because I'd been having quite the illicit affair with radiation lately, between mammograms and MRIs, not to mention the fun, "let's inject you with radioactive dye that will show up on our little Geiger counter" experiment.

Young hygienist Brittany made a note in my chart that I declined and informed me that I had a six-month reprieve before they would "require" me to have them.

OK, we got through that. I wasn't going to worry about six months from now; my goal was to get through today.

Cleaning complete, the dentist stopped by to do his 30-second exam.

Miss Brittany informed him of my reluctance to do X-rays. He asked why. "Is it a concern about money or time or radiation?"

"It's the radiation. I've had a lot of X-rays lately," I vaguely replied.

"Oh, that shouldn't be a worry. Brittany, where is the radiation chart," he asked.

As she looked around for the missing visual aid, I explained, "Look, I have breast cancer and am in between treatments. I didn't want it in my chart because I don't want to be asked about it every time I come here."

At this point, Brittany's face resembled a cow's that had stumbled upon a new gate and she glanced down at the floor.

The dentist said, "First of all, I'm sorry, and we really should put that in your chart because that's important, but we'll put in a note not to bring it up."

"Great, you do that," I thought. Instead, I just nodded and muttered, "thanks."

He then proceeded to show me the radiation chart that Brittany handed to him and pointed to the tiny little dental X-ray bar on the graph indicating radiation levels and began explaining how little radiation is in them.

I looked at the graph and noticed the bar for mammograms and MRIs (which is quite high) and pointed to those bars and said, "Understood, but here's what I've had lately and I will have more in the near future and I don't need a dental X-ray to add to it, thanks."

Really?! I have to argue with my dentist?

Now I understand what they mean by "battling breast cancer" because so many things feel like a battle.

Don't they get it? This is serious stuff! I understand a dental X-ray is just a small amount of radiation in the grand scheme of things. But a raindrop is just a small amount of water in a five-gallon bucket, but if it rains all day, the bucket will overflow.

Why must I explain this? I declined their X-ray. I was paying the bill, they work for me. I shouldn't have to explain why I declined. And after I politely explained why I declined, why did we have to continue to argue over this?

Suffice to say, I quickly found a new dentist.

I think all medical professionals should be better trained for this kind of situation. Perhaps a big, pink sticker could be placed on the front of our charts to let them know we are cancer patients/survivors. Because when you have cancer in your history, you probably become super sensitive to EVERYTHING and any casual sideways look by a doctor or any new question asked by a physician could become something to panic about, even if it's nothing.

Having a sticker to alert staff and having staff trained to be sensitive to those things would help greatly.

Your takeaway: You can say "no" to anything. You shouldn't have to provide a reason. You definitely shouldn't need to argue. If you aren't comfortable with your healthcare provider, find a new one. Get a second opinion. You well-being comes first!

15

"50 Shades of Gray" and Rita Wilson

"I'm so fancy. You already know. I'm in the fast lane from L.A. to Tokyo."

—*"Fancy" By Iggy Azalea*

I returned to my surgeon for a check-up. She looked at my breast. "Oh, you really bruised. I'm so sorry," she said.

I had to smile. Bruising wasn't a big concern of mine. Besides, I had noticed it went from a bright purple to a variation of colors.

"It's OK," I replied. "It's 50 shades of gray now. I'm feeling pretty trendy!"

(The fact was, the movie "50 Shades of Gray" was in the height of its popularity at the time.)

It had been three months since my diagnosis and if I thought I was alone in this, I'm not. Rita Wilson, an actress and the wife of Tom Hanks, was the latest famous person to announce she has breast cancer.

Of course, there are others, which I never paid much attention to, but by now am totally intrigued by each and every story. There is Amy Robach and Robin Roberts—both are in the media, so they captured my attention first. Being a music lover, I recalled Olivia

Newton-John. As a TV sitcom junkie, I always wanted to be one of kids on "Family Ties" and my TV mom, Meredith Baxter is a survivor. And I always wanted to be one of Charlie's Angels, and both Kate Jackson and Jaclyn Smith are survivors.

I'm in good company!

The key here is "survivors." People DO survive this disease!

It's easy to forget that when you are getting the sad looks and bad news and suffering through test after test.

No matter what your stage of diagnosis, there's always that reminder that this could be the end.

Very rarely do you hear about the survivors.

I stopped in at a local department store and was waiting in line when an elderly couple was talking to the sales clerk about their experience with cancer.

I interjected myself into their conversation (because, well, they were standing there in public holding up the line to have the chat) and mentioned my plight.

"Oh, honey, I'm a three-time cancer survivor," the woman said with a grin. "And just look at me!" (She look very healthy and well.)

She then offered to pray for me and invited me to her church, which I thought was very sweet.

I walked away from that exchange with hope.

I discovered you really have to focus on the success stories for your own well-being.

Your takeaway: Always have hope. Look for the success stories. Find a group of survivors, if that helps you, to share stories.

16

A Caped Crusader and a Soul Ride

Sorry, that's not in the job description.

At this point, my journey took an unexpected detour.

It wasn't the kind of detour that takes you along a pleasant country road where you discover a quaint little restaurant or shop you never would have found had you stayed the course.

No, this was the kind of detour where you followed the big orange sign, but then found yourself in the middle of nowhere with no idea where you are, nothing and no one around and no cell signal to use your GPS and, on top of that, you just drank a 20-ounce coffee and you have to pee!

THAT kind of a detour.

I was at work when I got the news. (Have I mentioned how much I appreciate the fact that I was able to work through this?)

It was bad news (does it ever end?!). I needed chemo. The cancer, while considered Stage 1, is the type that could return elsewhere and they wanted to prevent that.

At the time the oncologist called, I was covering an event in a Catholic school cafeteria. We were actually awarding a student for being an outstanding volunteer in her community. Our program was called "Caped Crusader." I gave a speech, presented her with a certificate and gave her a shiny, gold cape. It was a feel-good afternoon until the phone rang.

I believe that call was like that horrible day on Sept. 11, 2001—I doubt I will forget where I was when I found out.

Being told you need chemo is somehow worse than getting the cancer diagnosis—at least it was for me.

I mean, the subject had come up early on, but we didn't really think that was going to be necessary.

"How much are we talking," I asked.

"Six rounds. Eighteen weeks," Dr. Leah Cream responded.

It was April. She wanted to get things started right away. That meant my entire summer would be taken up with chemotherapy.

The entire summer. I had plans!

And ohmygosh, chemo! I was going to lose my hair.

I told her I would call the office to schedule my appointment and hung up, shell-shocked.

I looked around. Where was that damned Caped Crusader and why didn't she swoop in and save the day?!

I kept it together long enough to walk across the cafeteria, grab my assistant editor who had driven to this event, thank God, and told him I was ready to leave.

He grabbed his coat and followed me out of the school.

We got into his car, a Kia Soul, which was funny because well, I needed a little soul right then and there. I said, "Chris, I'm really sorry, but I'm going to cry right now. Please don't let it bother you. Don't file some HR suit because your boss is expecting you to tolerate her sobs. But I was just told I need chemotherapy."

He stopped buckling his seatbelt and looked at me. "Ohmygosh," he said. "Are you OK?"

I laughed out loud, because no, I was most definitely not OK.

We drove 12 miles back to the office talking as I dabbed my eyes with half-used tissues I had in my coat pocket.

He shared stories of women he knew that had been through cancer treatment and made it out the other side just fine.

It's funny, as bad as I felt, I felt more sorry for him because he certainly didn't get paid enough to have to deal with this.

I was so glad I wasn't alone. I was so grateful he drove that time, which was rare as I usually drove separately. That day, Christopher Hopkins was not just an assistant editor, he was a blessing.

He was the first person I told about the chemo. Next, I would have to tell my boss, then my family. This little cancer thing was turning into a bigger deal than I thought.

For some reason, the diagnosis and the surgery and even the idea of radiation didn't rattle me. But chemo, that's serious stuff.

Suddenly, in one phone call, I became a real victim.

I didn't really know what would happen next, but I was certain I wasn't going to like it.

Your takeaway: Don't ever take anything for granted. Expect the good, but prepare for the worst. And always, ALWAYS keep a fresh pack of tissues in your purse or pocket. You never know when you'll need them.

17

Dark Thoughts and Low Blows

"I'm friends with the monster that's under my bed, get along with the voices inside of my head, you're trying to save me, stop holding your breath and you think I'm crazy, yeah you think I'm crazy ... ."

—"The Monster" by Eminen with Rihanna

Again, my cancer diagnosis seemed to take a backseat to the anxiety I was feeling.

Every cough made me wonder if I was dying. Every ache and pain made me wonder, "is this cancer?"

My hip hurt one morning. I probably slept on it wrong. But panic ensued.

Some days, I could hold it together quite well. Other days, I wondered if I'd lost my bloody mind.

It was spring. It was allergy season. I have had seasonal allergies and take a daily prescription for it, but this particular morning, I awoke and blew my nose and it bled.

It lasted maybe five minutes, if that, and quickly resolved.

But my panic over the moment lasted far beyond the actual nose bleed.

OMG! My nose is bleeding. BLEEDING. I SEE BLOOD!!! What is wrong with me? Why is it doing this? Do I have a brain tumor?! Is this the beginning of the end?

I thought about getting on Google to see what could possibly cause it, but decided against it.

Taking a breath and stopping to think about it, I realized it was probably from dry air indoors combined with blowing too hard.

Next came "clickitis."

My thumb—the base of it at the joint—had been hurting off and on for a few days, then a week. As I drove home one evening, I began to panic. I had heard cancer can spread to the bone. Could I have bone cancer in my thumb?! Do I call the doctor? What on earth could be causing this pain?!

As I pondered my certain immediate demise, a "Hootie and the Blowfish" hit came on the radio. Now, I love Darius Rucker as much as the next country girl, but having to sit through 3:46 of his garbled attempt at rock, "I only wanna be with youuuuuuu" was more than I could handle in this moment of panic.

I pushed the black button on my steering wheel to get something—anything—else to come out of the speakers. An immediate pain shot through my thumb joint—the joint of the finger I had just used to change stations.

And just like that, I realized I had "clickitis" ... crisis averted.

I change radio stations and CD tracks as frequently as the second-hand digit changes on my LED dashboard clock. Apparently, that nasty habit has taken its toll on my thumb joint. Whew! I'm not dying! ... from this at least.

But "the worst" is where my mind tended to go these days, because I'd had a lot of "the worst" at that point.

Actually, my "worst" wasn't really the worst in comparison to what some people with this awful disease must endure. I knew this, but thus far, my world had been rocked far beyond my worst nightmare.

I began to wonder if I was nuts. I'm began to think it's not the cancer that will get me, it's the crazy.

But it's not just the medical issues that are throwing me into a sea of bad thoughts.

I mean, I wasn't afraid of dying, per se, because once that happens, I won't care.

But my family will care.

And that's what made me cry.

As I said before, I had my ups and downs, but it seemed like every day was something new.

Some days, I could push it from my mind and actually enjoy my day. Other times, I threw one heck of a pity party. I never invited anyone and no one ever attended, it was always just me, and how pathetic is a pity party of one?

Remember that old "Partridge Family" theme song, "C'mon get happy"?

I so wanted to get happy, but sometimes, I couldn't make the effort.

And it was so hard to get away from reminders.

Take Facebook, for example.

Apparently, someone there monitors posts pretty carefully because I didn't post much about my diagnosis, but at some point, my feed started providing pop-ups about cancer stories and advertisements. That's not cool, FB, not cool!

Before my diagnosis, I had never paid attention to how much cancer is out there in the media.

But after being diagnosed, it seemed like every magazine I picked up had a story in it, even though it wasn't October.

I thought I was safe picking up a "Cosmo" that highlighted stories on the cover about how to have a great orgasm and please your man in bed.

I guess every woman could use this advice and I was no different and maybe I'd learn a thing or two while escaping my sad reality, but nope!

Right after an article on sexual positions, I turned a page to find a story about a woman fighting lymphoma.

That was a low blow even for "Cosmo"!

Speaking of relationships, at this point, I'd been dating a man for less than a year. We got along quite well and had so much fun together. I knew he was "the one," but I don't think he had figured that out yet.

I kept a lot of the things going on with my health to myself because that is certainly not what he signed up for when he created the profile that caught my eye on Match.com.

He knew my diagnosis, but I kept assuring him that it was no big deal and everything would be fine.

We weren't living together at the time of my treatments. We lived an hour apart and he worked out of town through the week, so we would take turns staying at one of our houses on the weekends.

That had advantages because when I was feeling sorry for myself and just wanted to be alone, I could be. But the downside was when I wanted someone there, I was alone.

Of course, he would have dropped everything to come stay with me had I asked him. But how do you explain to your partner that you are afraid and don't want to be alone?

I had assigned him one task: to keep things "normal" for me. He constantly reassured me during my crying fits that everything would be OK.

But truth be told, I was having a bit of an existential crisis with the relationship.

What would the future hold? How would we spend the rest of our lives? How could I make any promises to someone when I didn't know if I would have another year or two or 10?

Is that fair to do to someone?

I had a very hard time showing anyone my fears, because to me, that was to be weak and I wasn't supposed to be weak.

People at work kept telling me how strong I was.

But I wasn't strong.

I was scared as hell.

I didn't know what the future would hold. I didn't know if I had a future.

But how could I vocalize that to someone I loved?

I think I didn't want to see fear reflected in someone else's eyes because that would make my fear legitimate.

Sometimes, my best attempts to keep my fears from my family failed.

There was one particular rough day when work was particularly challenging and all I could think about was starting chemo and losing my hair and being sick. I didn't want to be sick!

Of course, that was the day when my daughter called to complain about her allergies.

She was at college and she wanted advice on getting her medication (the college physician gave her a prescription) and I think, some motherly sympathy.

Granted, she sounded all congested and miserable as soon as I picked up the phone.

Unfortunately, she caught me at a time when I wasn't feeling particularly sympathetic to anyone's plight but my own.

I tried to be nice, but all I could think of was, "Really?! You're worrying about a stuffy nose, when I'm about to have massive chemicals pumped into my body and lose all my hair?!"

Of course, I didn't say that to her, but I guess my lack of sympathy was conveyed in the shortness of my tone because later, I received a text that said, "You've been weird … apathetic."

Ya think?!

Forgive me, sweetheart. I *so* want to be "normal"!

But right now, I've got a lot on my plate.

I wanted to pretend things were OK because if I convinced myself I was OK, maybe I would be OK.

I don't know if that was right or wrong, but it got me through it.

Looking back, I probably should have been more open to showing my emotions.

But that was a lesson I hadn't learned yet.

There were a lot of lessons I hadn't mastered at the time, but have since come to learn.

Take death.

Apparently, I couldn't have a day without thinking about my demise, because one day, my ex-husband was in a car crash.

Fortunately, he was fine. His truck didn't fare so well, but that's no big deal.

Our daughter went to pick him up after the crash.

She called to tell me.

I hung up the phone and panicked.

He could have been killed! What if he was killed and I died and our only child was left an orphan?

OK, so she was almost 21 at the time, but we are very close!

This was too much to process! I thought, "Really, God?! I don't need this much drama in my life."

Some of the drama, I guess I asked for.

I finally had the opportunity to share my diagnosis with two family members who aren't close family, but were at one time. We were chatting on social media.

One ignored me completely. She didn't even respond and I know she got the message because it was marked "seen."

The other did reply to a different part of the conversation, but failed to address my cancer in any way.

I don't know why I was surprised.

In one case, the family member is related to another family member who, when I had a miscarriage years ago, called to ask if she could borrow my crib, since I obviously wouldn't be needing it. (Yes, that really did happen!)

Apparently, the age-old "I'm sorry" or "Is there anything I can do?" is lost on people these days.

Even a "Gee, I don't know what to say" would have sufficed.

I guess I'd just have to get over it.

I had to get some control.

As Miss Smith used to say during times like these, "Go collect yourself."

I never could figure out how any of us second-graders could actually "collect" ourselves, but our generation would probably instruct others to "get a grip."

And so I figured I'd start with something I could control.

As the medical bills continued to add up, I began thinking about my finances. I had been wanting to get things in order and pay off debts anyway, so I decided to take out a loan to consolidate my credit card debt.

My credit union advertised that application was easy over the phone and, if approved, all I would have to do was visit a local branch and sign papers.

Fortunately, I was approved.

I headed to the bank over my lunch hour and the loan officer had the papers ready for me to sign. This was indeed going to be easy!

Of course, you are offered all kinds of options with your loan, including disability/death insurance for a small premium. I decided to opt for that because, well, at this point, that could come in handy!

As I read through it, pen in hand, about to sign, I saw the disclaimer: "If you've been diagnosed with cancer in the past two years, you are ineligible."

Seriously?!

Now, I had to admit that and have the loan officer reprint the paperwork and initial that I am ineligible.

Geesh, I can't even go to the freakin' bank without being reminded that I have cancer!

I felt like I should wear a sweater with a big, pink "C" on it.

Your takeaway: It's easy to feel sorry for yourself. It's OK to feel sad or angry or scared. You have to do what you are comfortable with. But consider that it really is OK to admit fear. And think about allowing those close to you to comfort you. And keep your expectations of others in check. Don't let them get to you.

18

Help Me, Wanda. Help, Help Me, Wanda!

Apparently, life stops at the point of diagnosis.

All tests results back, my treatment plan is announced: 18 weeks of chemo (six treatments, one every three weeks) beginning Friday, April 24, which happened to be my ex-husband's birthday. Well, I guess I will never forget either date.

Funny story, when I shared that coincidence with one member of my medical team, she shared that it was also her ex-husband's birthdate. We quickly compared notes to make certain that we did not, indeed, share the same ex-husband, too.

During the chemo and for one year following, I would also receive via IV a drug called Herceptin.

After the regular chemo, it would be five weeks of daily radiation and a daily estrogen-blocking pill for five to 10 years.

BUT all that gives me a 90 percent chance it won't return in the next five years, I'm told.

Yes, I will lose my hair, but hopefully, thanks to modern medicine, I won't be sick or overwhelmingly tired.

I've got age on my side, my doctor said. I foundd that to be a small consolation, as I'd have much preferred to suffer at age 80, but … .

So, by my October birthday, I would be almost as good as new! And that was six months away.

Enter Wanda, the oncologist's nurse, who I could tell was going to become my new bestie.

She, I was instructed, would be my first point of contact with my oncologist.

I'm not sure that my relationship with Wanda got off on the right foot, however.

Few of the medical facilities I used allowed you to do your own scheduling. Some nurse was always on my phone telling me when my next appointment would be. They just booked them, like I had nothing better to do that sit around and wait for the next appointment.

I had a job! I had things to do!

Each and every time, the nurses (most of whom were congenial) seemed shocked when I said, "No, that won't work for me." Some were even left momentarily speechless.

Wanda was one of them to bear the brunt of my righteous indignation early on when she called to schedule a test.

Wanda told me, in her always chipper voice, when the appointment would take place. It happened to be at a time in the middle of the day on a day when I had work deadlines. I informed her, politely, but firmly, that that time wouldn't work.

I must have been the first patient to ever say no because Wanda was rendered speechless for a minute.

Hey, some of us have work and deadlines and important stuff booked with our children! Seriously. There was no way I was gonna rearrange my entire life if I didn't have to. My goal was to maintain as much normalcy as possible.

Wanda was able to reschedule the appointment and did so with cheer and grace. Most of the time, others were able to schedule around my schedule.

But I found this odd on the several occasions it occurred.

Do people just say "yes" and accept the inconvenient appointment? The world may never know ….

Wanda and I went on to have a very good relationship. I called her many times over the course of my treatment and she was always there to help. I grinned each time because in my head, I always heard my version of the Beach Boys classic, "Help me, Rhonda."

Takeaway: This is YOUR life and YOUR schedule. Make them work around you when you can. Not only will it help with the ongoing disruption to your life, it will help you feel in control.

19

My Friends and Family Plan

"I get by with a little help from my friends."

—*"With a Little Help From My Friends"*
by The Beatles

As I sat in a doctor's office waiting for my appointment, I noticed a woman enter the lobby. She had an adorable haircut and reminded me of someone I used to know and I had to do a double-take to make sure it wasn't her.

She crossed to the reception desk and began conversing with Nicole, the patient advocate I had met who I really liked.

From across the room, I could hear their conversation. They were talking about the frustration of traffic and how the woman was searching for a massage therapist to help her through some stiffness she was having after her mastectomy.

I knew from her traffic description that she had to live someone in my direction and I had a great massage therapist.

So I walked over and inserted myself into their discussion because, well, I figured it was nothing personal or it wouldn't have been broadcast across the office waiting room.

I introduced myself to her and told her about my massage therapist.

She told me where she lived. I was surprised because we lived in the same small town, about 45 minutes from our doctor's office.

I asked her where in the town she lived.

As it turned out, her home was literally across the field from my house in an adjacent neighborhood, yet we had never met.

We exchanged emails.

Jennifer went on to become my cancer buddy. We were about a week apart in our treatment and from that point on, exchanged emails and texts and phone calls.

She has been such a blessing in my life!

She gave me strength and we talked about things you only can talk about with someone else who is going through what you are going through.

I can't tell you how invaluable this relationship was during my treatment. I don't know how I'd have gotten though it without her. She was my pink angel!

I had a few of those "meet cutes" during that time.

My boyfriend and I were at the airport waiting to fly out when I noticed an older couple in line in front of us.

The petite woman was carrying a bag that had a big pink ribbon keychain dangling from the handle. I thought it said "survivor" on it.

I was looking for good news and validation anywhere I could get it at the time, so I asked her. "Excuse me, I noticed your bag. Are you a cancer survivor," I said.

She replied that she was and that was 20 years ago and she was doing great.

We chatted a bit after that.

She didn't know it, but in that brief airport conversation, she became my mentor. I decided I was going to live another 20 years!

Your takeaway: Don't be shy! Step out of your comfort zone sometimes and talk to people. Make a friend. Find someone to share your journey! If you are a spiritual person, ask God to lead you to your angel. He will.

20

Look Good, Feel Better!

"Just do it."

—*Nike*

By now, I was tasked with having an echocardiogram—an ultrasound of the heart. Apparently, your heart has to be in tip-top shape in order to get some types of chemo.

It was an easy test and I came through it with flying colors.

I also decided to consult with a cancer specialist who also happens to be a holistic doctor about how my diet can help me get through treatment.

After discussing fresh fruits and vegetables and some supplements, I stopped at the grocery store and spent $115 on healthy food—which really isn't a lot for one week, if you factor in breakfast, lunch and dinner.

It's basically no caffeine, no sugar, no processed food, no red meat—healthy stuff that I should be eating anyhow.

I was halfway through Day One when all I could think about was food.

I had long-grain rice with vegetables and baked chicken for lunch and a handful of grapes.

As I sat in my office, I looked at the pink post-it note stuck to my computer screen that reminded me about a deadline and thought, "Wow. That's the color of a strawberry-frosted Dunkin' Donut and OMG do I want one!"

I considered a DD run because it's right down the street from my office and, well, I'd only been trying this healthy eating stuff for one day, so it'd be OK to ease myself into it, right?!

But I knew I shouldn't.

I re-focused on work, only to realize I was tired. Like suddenly dog tired.

"Why am I suddenly so tired?" I wondered, looking at the empty bowl of healthy food, rather than empty carbs.

Then I remembered I had switched to decaf tea—green decaf tea—that morning.

Something told me it was going to be a long few weeks!

But I wanted to do whatever I could to mitigate the effects of chemotherapy.

At this point, it had been three months since I had a biopsy and was told it was likely cancer. I knew I was facing chemo. I knew I'd lose my hair.

The thought of that was more than I could handle, so I went and got a wig in preparation.

It was a difficult thing for me to do, but thanks to the American Cancer Society, I got a beautiful wig for free! And, frankly, it was much nicer than my own thin hair—it even had highlights that I didn't have to sit foil-wrapped in a chair for.

A lovely volunteer named Linda helped me to pick it out.

While waiting in the cancer center for Linda to be ready, I met a couple—the wife was undergoing chemo and, as it turned out, they were from the town next to mine. I found that oddly comforting.

I also signed up to attend the Look Good, Feel Better class sponsored by the local chapter of the American Cancer Society.

The class is for women with any kind of cancer and offers make-up tips and scarf tying instruction and almost any other piece of instruction you need for maintaining a beauty regimen while you go through cancer treatment.

Radiation can make your skin dry. Chemo can cause hair to fall out, including eyebrows and eyelashes.

I wanted to be ready for anything.

As we went around the table to introduce ourselves, a woman who looked vaguely familiar looked at me and said, "I remember you from Gymboree."

Gymboree?

It had been almost 20 years since I took my daughter to the mother-child play group.

When she said her name, I then recognized it (we both had unusual last names).

We compared notes – her daughter was a year behind mine in college, but, oddly, they were both at the same university.

It really is a small world!

Again, having a friendly face in a very scary place helped immensely.

There were about a dozen ladies in that room that night, all facing different types and stages of cancer. We were all frightened, not knowing exactly what would happen to our bodies.

But we all wanted to beat this.

The first thing you do when you go into battle is gear-up.

We all knew the wonderful samples of blush and eyeliner weren't going to make us better, but they might help to make us "normal." And some days, that's the best you can hope for.

Your takeaway: Whether it's diet tips or make-up tips, think about what might make you feel better even when you don't feel good. Seek that help. You'll feel better for it.

21

"Obama" Joins My Chemo Administration

"Yes, we can!"

—P<small>RES</small>. B<small>ARACK</small> O<small>BAMA</small>

I'll be honest, when I found out I'd have to get a medi-port inserted into my chest in order to receive chemotherapy, I was more than a little scared. It would be placed in my upper chest and inserted into my jugular vein and remain under the skin.

I mean, they are sticking something in your chest that will be there for at least six months and, in my case, a year. Not only is that symbolic of just how long my life is going to be disrupted, it's a constant reminder that I'm not well.

I had so many questions and concerns.

Will you be able to see it? Will it be bothersome? And, well, they're going to have to INSERT it into my CHEST!

No worries, they told me, they'd put me under using something that sounded rather delightful: "twilight anesthesia." I'm thinking moonlight, a warm summer breeze and crickets chirping (that's how it sounded, rather than what it actually was, which was more like more like "Twilight"—but we'll get to that soon enough).

I got to the hospital bright and early one Wednesday morning and waited to be prepped. All they'd need to do, they said, was take some blood and insert an IV, then they'd take me down to radiology for the procedure.

Unfortunately, I was not to drink anything after midnight, so my tiny, shy veins were easily able to hide due to lack of fluids. It took two nurses and a member of the IV Team an hour and a half to insert the IV and draw blood.

At my hospital, the IV Team is able to insert the IV, but not do a blood draw—which, in my case, required a different vein.

Anyway, I finally arrived in Cardiovascular and Interventional Radiology, where Dr. Harjit Singh did a 2-second ultrasound of my neck and pronounced, "I will be the only man to tell you this, but you have a beautiful jugular."

That made me grin. At least I had that going for me.

Next thing I knew, I was moving onto the operating table, strapped down and a hair net, oxygen line and face mask was placed.

The nurse said, "I'm just gonna give you some oxygen" which immediately made me think of that '70s song, "Love is like oxygen, you get too much, you get too high, not enough and you're gonna die" and so I told the whole OR crew, who laughed and Dr. Singh began singing.

Any doctor who knows the lyrics to some '70s tune and is willing to belt it out in front of his patient and team is A-OK with me!

The nurse then informed me that I would be awake during the procedure.

Wait right there! AWAKE? While they puncture my jugular vein and insert something foreign into my chest?! Are you FREAKIN KIDDING ME?!

They were not.

"Don't worry, you will know what's going on, but you won't care," Dr. Singh assured me.

And you know what? He was right. I was awake, I think, for the entire time. I knew they were working, but couldn't feel it. They had a drape up between my head and chest, so I couldn't see, either, which reminded me of my C-section years ago.

In under a half-hour, it was done.

I spent two hours in recovery—a requirement of my hospital—but I got some food and juice and left to go home. No pain and just two bandages.

Later, I got a slight rash—likely an allergy to the bandages, which I'm notorious for.

I don't know why I was so worried about port implantation.

I slept like a baby that night and woke up the next morning feeling fine—until I sat up to get out of bed and discovered it was sore, but two Tylenol kept that at bay.

My friend who had recently gotten her port called me that night. She told me she named her port.

I thought about that. What would I name something I didn't want, would prove to be irritating and I was stuck with for a year?

There was only one answer: Obama.

Your takeaway: Don't sweat the scary stuff. Trust in your doctors. Find humor when you can (even if it's at the expense of the sitting President).

22

Chemo: Round One

"Don't think about what can happen in a month. Don't think about what can happen in a year. Just focus on the 24 hours in front of you and do what you can to get closer to where you want to be."

—Eric Thomas

My ex-husband's birthday and my first chemo had finally arrived. My mother and I entered the cancer center and were led to an entire wing of little rooms where patients were given IV treatments. We were escorted to our own room which had a bathroom attached. I thought that would come in handy if I got sick.

I was instructed to stay hydrated and so I drank plenty of tea and water before I left the house and carried a water bottle into the hospital.

You can read below exactly what occurred during treatment.

The first one was intimidating because you know you're getting heavy drugs put into your body and you're not sure how you will react. Will there be an allergy? Will I get sick?

It's scary stuff!

My mom and I talked the entire time and watched a little TV over the nearly five hours we were there.

The nurses encouraged us to eat something, so my mom went to the hospital cafeteria and brought back sandwiches. I was surprised eating was allowed.

And then, it was time to go home and wait for the effects.

I will share with you what my treatments were like, although not everyone's treatment is the same.

Here's what happened each of the six times:

I had a port in my chest, so there were no IVs needed for my chemo.

When I arrived at the hospital, they inserted a line into my port. The first time, it felt as if they stuck a thumb tack into my chest, but it only stung for a second.

Next, they handed me what they called "pre-meds," which, in my case, was a handful of anti-nausea pills and an Ativan to calm my nerves.

After that, they hung the chemo bags from an IV pole and ran the line into the port. I didn't feel a thing.

They hung one bag at a time and each drug took a different length of time to drip into my system.

While the bags dripped, I read or did crossword puzzles (thanks, Colleen!) or watched TV. As it happened, re-runs of "Charlie's Angels" came on at 10 a.m. every Friday, so I made a habit of tuning in.

I loved watching those shows as a kid and watching them now just made me feel good.

I also made sure to drink at least two or three bottles of something (water, iced tea, milk) during treatment and I usually ate lunch, too, thanks to the hospital cafeteria and snack bar.

I have to say, I almost enjoyed these days (well, as much as you can enjoy getting chemo in a hospital ward). I found them relaxing and almost empowering, knowing I was killing cancer cells.

When the bags were empty, the buzzer beeped and a nurse changed them.

At the end, the nurse pulled the line out of my port and I drove home.

The first two treatments, someone went with me to chemo. The rest, I went alone.

I was very fortunate, I'm told. I was able to drive. Some people are tired at the end or feel nauseous, but I didn't, and that was my experience with chemo days all of the six times.

During my chemotherapy, I kept a journal so I would know what to expect with the next treatment and be able to look back at some point to see how far I had come.

Here is the entry from the first treatment and subsequent days:

Day of chemo: Felt great. Drank LOTS of water.
Day 2: Felt great, went out to dinner.
Day 3: Felt tired, slept off and on in afternoon. Warm foods don't sit very well.
Day 4: Felt OK, not sure if I'd be tired or not. Afternoon napped.
Day 5: Felt A-OK, except for severe constipation. I was instructed to do what amounted to a colon cleanse, as if prepping for a colonoscopy. That was fun ... not.
Day 6: Felt great, except it's now that time of the month.
Day 7: My tongue feels burned. My throat feels burned. I can't stand to eat hot stuff or drink tea. Getting random pain

in my back kidney area. Hoping this is either coincidence or the heels I'm wearing.

Day 8: Noticed the back pain is worse upon doing stairs, kind of like spasms. I am able to drink/eat warm stuff.

Day 9: My nose has dried out and so has, apparently, everything else. Still having digestive issues. Been walking as much as possible and drinking water.

Days 10-11: Still stuffy. Throat still sore. Tongue getting better. Appetite is normal.

Day 14: Returned from lunch to get sick. Thought I had food poisoning. Got worse overnight. Back hurt so bad I couldn't sleep, then started puking.

Day 15: Woke up to find my hair falling out in gentle handfuls. Funny how this happened all of a sudden, just when I thought I wasn't going to lose it.

Day 16 (Mother's Day): Finally went to ER: I have a kidney stone which, they say, is unrelated to chemo, but I wonder if it's because I've been drinking so much when I usually drink very little. The good news is my blood counts were pretty darned good when they drew it. Hair is still gently wafting onto my shoulders, the table I am eating at and down my arms.

Day 17: Woke up and still have hair on my head. Surprised it wasn't all over my pillow as everyone told me to expect. Instead, standing up was like a gentle rain of hair down my back and shoulders. Lovely. It was Monday. Figured I'd wear the wig to work, as people may have forgotten over the weekend how thin my natural hair is and may not notice. That plan sorta worked!

 Daughter doesn't like wig.

Had lunch with a survivor. She told me about compression hose and tear duct drains to prevent scars. This I will investigate. *More on this later.*

Day 18: Still have hair on my head (no clue how or why, being that it's still dropping—coincidentally like those "helicopter" things that are falling from the maple tree onto my roof). It's great not to have to wash and dry my hair in the morning, but I don't like wearing wigs. It doesn't feel natural and I'm constantly worried it will slip askew.

We're to get gusty winds today—30 to 40 mph expected. My boss said when I am ready to leave please let him know so he can charge up his camera phone and walk me out.

He's such a card! He should be dealt with.

PS: I'm still waiting for the kidney stone to pass.

Let me say I am grateful for modern medicine. I just wish I wouldn't have had to use it. And you know what's really sad? When you go to the oncology infusion floor where so many people are receiving heavy-duty drugs and they've lost hair and weight and don't know their outcomes, but yet you no longer feel intimidate or frightened by it. I actually got to the point where I looked forward to going for chemo treatment because I knew I was killing cancer cells. I knew in the four hours I had to sit there as medication dripped into my veins, that I would be taken care of. If I was cold, someone would bring me a warm blanket. If I got thirsty, someone would bring me a drink. There was a young man on the infusion floor named Sam, who came around every Friday to ask if I needed anything. I looked forward to his visit because I knew there wasn't much I could have asked for that he wouldn't have tried his best to bring me.

I got into the habit of stopping by the hospital cafeteria before my treatment to pick up lunch or a snack and drink. I always brought magazines, so I would page through the current issues as I watched re-runs of "Charlie's Angels" and "The Golden Girls."

You wouldn't think going to chemo could be something you don't dread, but I didn't.

And a shoutout to every single nurse on that unit: You are all fabulous. I wrote down many of your names, but I didn't want to forget anyone, so I won't call you each out. But thank you!

Your takeaway: Your experience may be different than mine, but you've got to take each day as it comes and look ahead one day at a time. Live from treatment to treatment. Do what you feel up to between treatments. Keep a journal. It will help you and your doctor remember things to discuss. And seriously, drink lots of water!

23

Let's Talk About The Hair

"Oh where is my hairbrush? Oh where is my hairbrush? Oh, where, oh, where, oh, where, oh, where, oh, where, oh, where, oh, where, oh, where oh, where ... is my hairbrush?"

—*"The Hairbrush Song by Veggie Tales*

The hair loss was definitely the hardest part of chemo for me, because that's when you realize nothing is "normal" anymore. You are reminded every time you look into the mirror.

But don't fret!

My hair began to seriously fall out about three weeks after my first chemo. I had been waiting for the piles on the pillow that I was warned to expect, but I had nothing like that.

Instead, mine seemed to prefer dropping out over the sink as I applied makeup and in the tub. Some friends who had been through treatment told me to just shave it, but I refused because I wanted to know exactly how much I'd lose and how long it would take (if you are going through this now, does your youngest kid need a science project this year? haha).

Anyhow, one day, weeks later, the wonderful man in my life walked in from work and handed me a bag filled with something he picked up at lunch. No, it wasn't a coral pin or a jade bracelet to make me feel better (if you're a "Brady Bunch" fan, you'll get the reference).

It was this plastic stick thing you use to clear a drain of hair.

I thought, "What the heck is this? Are you even serious? Come on, dude! Who presents such a thing during a time when I am already horrified that I've lost so much hair down the drain?"

But he was so proud of his purchase.

I realized how for a man who is used to fixing things that go wrong and he can't fix this, to him, it was his contribution to fixing a problem.

Man logic! God love him!

In his defense, I had hidden much of my hair loss from him. You probably wonder how that's possible, since we do share a bed.

But I chose to always wear a scarf to bed from as soon as I started losing hair.

And at some point, I ditched the scarves and just started wearing a wig to bed. I couldn't see myself as normal in a scarf. At least I looked normal when I got up in the morning with the wig.

I wore a wig from early on to work as well.

I picked a Monday to debut the wig and slid into one of my favorite, most flattering dresses.

As I walked down the hallway at work, one of the guys hollered, "Hey, you got your hair done!"

I chuckled. "No, not really," I said as I stopped to chat with him. "It's a wig."

"NO WAY," he said. "Really?! It looks like your hair, only puffier."

I had to laugh at that. I mean, he was right.

"So how much hair have you lost," he wondered.

I told him I still had some, but it's so thin I figured I may as well get used to the wig.

I wore the wig for weeks before most of my other colleagues noticed. It really was a color and style similar to my own.

About every week or so for the first two months, my curious colleague would inquire about my hair loss amounts.

You may think that is rude or annoying or just way too personal for someone at work to say and do. But we were a pretty tight group of co-workers and I found it oddly comforting, mainly because I, too, was curious about this whole hair loss process and he always made me feel better because he was interested and brave enough to ask.

He always had something encouraging to say, too, the whole way through my treatments, always checking in to make sure I was OK.

Twice, I took him aside, removed the wig and showed him my balding/bald head. He was the only person I shared that with the entire time.

You may wonder why I didn't allow my boyfriend to see me bald. I just couldn't. With my colleague, there were no expectations. He was a friend at work and I didn't care if he found me attractive or not.

My partner, on the other hand, I wanted him to find me attractive. I did't want him to have that memory of me bald in his head. I knew he wouldn't care. He had told me he didn't care.

It wasn't about him. It was about me.

I wore my wig all the time. And I mean ALL the time. I took it off to shower or when we rode the motorcycle (and then I kept it in a purse in the saddlebag in case we went somewhere where I wanted to remove my do-rag).

Life with a wig could be challenging.

For example, I was warned not to expose the wig to heat, for fear it might melt. So every time I baked something in the oven, I had to ask a family member to remove the dish because I didn't want to melt my hair.

When we took a trip to Walt Disney World, we were at a resort standing with a group of my boyfriend's colleagues and it was getting dark, so the resort turned on those tall heaters that radiate heat from above.

As we all gathered around the heat, I suddenly remembered what was on my head and had to step away from the group and the heater so as not to bippity-boppity-burn my wig!

Speaking of my boyfriend, bless his heart, he is a big little boy. He likes his toys and prefers them shiny and with wheels.

Concerned that maybe I wouldn't be able to ride on the back of his motorcycle that summer, he used that as an excuse to buy a used 1990-something Mazda Miata convertible. He was so excited to offer another weekend of keeping things "normal" by taking off under sunny skies with the top down.

The grin on his face when he backed it out of the garage had to have been as big as it was when he was 10 on Christmas morning.

As I stood in the driveway looking at the tiny topless two-seater, my only thought was, "Well, shit. How am I going to keep a wig on my head going 55 mph?"

I mean, the motorcycle was great because I put on a do-rag then strapped on a helmet and we were good to go.

But this, this was gonna take some creativity!

I didn't want to harsh his mellow, so I grabbed a ball cap, tightened it over my wig and climbed in.

The entire time we rode, I kept a hand close to my head just in case I felt the wind tug my head dressings.

I mean, imagine driving down the interstate and having to say, "Hey, honey, can you pull over, my hair just blew off?"

My strategy worked. We took off many times in that little car and I didn't lose my wig once!

Your takeaway: It's OK to mourn the loss of your hair. It's OK to be proud and sport the bald style. Everyone is different when it comes to this part of the situation. And when it comes to our partners, I think it's harder for them sometimes than it is for us. And finally, you have to allow those you love to clean the drain now and then—literally and figuratively. Hang in there!

Also: most men are clueless. Seriously. Clueless. They can't help this. We just have to stay two steps ahead!

24

My Chemo Journal Highlights

"If you're going through hell, keep on going, don't slow down, if you're scared, don't show it you might get out before the devil even knows you're there."

—*"If You're Going Through Hell by Rodney Atkins*

At the risk of boring you with every little detail of my journey, I will share the highlights of my chemo treatments, so you have some perspective of what my treatment was like and some of the issues that came up along the way.

Please remember that your journey may be different. Also, remember I'm not qualified to provide you with medical advice. Talk to your doctor with any concerns you may have.

I just want you to have some idea of what you could be in for. These are entries from my journal at the time:

Second chemo treatment: went well.
Day 1: went to a wedding. Aside from kidney stone, felt fine.
Day 2 after second: tired. Slept most of afternoon. Finally passed the kidney stone! Yay!

Day 3 after treatment: feel woozy, like I can't quite get my reflexes to function correctly. Almost like I've had a drink or two. Ick. At work. Probably shouldn't be. Is it too soon to say I'm kinda tired of this?

Day 4: still feel nauseated most of the day. No appetite for anything except homemade spaghetti. How odd. Also think I have bladder infection. Starting antibiotics. Still have strange feeling in my back from time to time.

Day 5: Feeling less nauseated, but still not right. Still on spaghetti kick. Thinking now it's the antibiotics.

Day 6: Still feeling not right, but better.

Day 7: Feeling normal. Except now I have a yeast infection from antibiotics. Ugh. Done with spaghetti kick now. Tongue starting to feel burnt again. Hair still falling out in handfuls (but I refuse to shave it!)—like little piles on the floor of the bathroom. Ick.

Day 8: hiked a bit today. Feel fine.

Day 9: hiked a more strenuous trail today. Feel fine.

Day 10: Feel fine. My nose is dry again. Eyes watering.

Day 11: bacterial infection. Ugh. On antibiotics.

Day 14: Tongue still feels a bit burnt, taste is still off a bit. No more nausea!

Day 17: (same)

Will I ever be "normal" again?

Third treatment down!

Went well.

Day 1: felt fine. Worked the Central Penn Parent Family Festival

Day 2: walked 3 miles in the morning, tired, but not exhausted, in afternoon. Slept a bit.

Day 3: felt OK, just a bit unmotivated. Constipated. Again. Worked from home because they prescribed a colon cleanse—the high-test kind like you do before a colonoscopy. It took that much to liberate my bound-up system. This is so not cool!

I took one little nap. Up half the night. Mouth feels dry/burnt again and nothing tastes good. Not even iced tea.

Day 4: went to work. Shoulda stayed home. Tired.

Fourth down!
Day 1: Felt fine
Day 2: felt OK. Still coughing from leftover bronchitis. Constipated.
Day 3: Felt slightly tired.
Day 4: Felt extremely nauseated. All thought of food and drink made me sick.
Day 5: Still queasy. Muscles hurt, esp legs. Not even drinks appeal.
Day 6: Able to eat reasonably well, though picky. Still craving chicken and stuff with red sauce. Sweets are a major turnoff. Don't feel like drinking either. Ugh.
Day 7/8: Feeling much better stomach-wise, but now have rash on face. Muscles (especially legs) still feel odd, especially after climbing stairs.
Day 10: Have that thing in the back again where my muscles throb after a quick movement. Eyes still runny. Still have rash, which doctor says is allergic reaction to something.
Day 11. Rash still red. Leg muscles still achy. Fingernails hurt. They say this is all side effect of chemo (and not an allergy like I thought). This sucks.

Number five.
So this was different: When your attending nurse (who is expecting a call from your doctor) gets off the phone, throws her hands up in the air and says, "Am I on Candid Camera?!" you can assume it's not a good thing. Turns out the medication on my chart was the wrong dosage and she caught it, although it took several phone calls to get things set straight. I love each and every one of those nurses on the cancer unit!

Day 1: Felt great.

Day 2: felt great. Went to Amish Country; started to feel nauseated that night.

Day 3: Tired. Nauseated.

Day 4: Horribly constipated. Thought of eating OR drinking made me nauseated. Slept off and on all day.

Day 5: Meh.

Day 6: I feel almost normal! Red moons on my fingernails now and they are painful. Fingers are swollen, I think.

Day 17: Have been feeling pretty good! But my fingernails still hurt (I think I'm gonna lose the nails) and I'm retaining water in my ankles and, apparently, in my thighs.

Day 18: Ankles still swollen. Sandals are snug. Rings are tight. WTH?

Sixth and last!
Day 1: felt fine (steroids took care of edema on ankles!)

Day 2: felt fine

Day 3: tired, slightly nauseous

Day 4: slightly nauseous; little light-headed; constipated, despite laxatives

Day 5: still constipated. Horribly. Feel bloated and awful.

Day 6: feeling better, just appetite and taste off. Tongue feels burned again.
Day 8: have the face rash back on my right cheek. Just like before. Ugh.
Day13: Several of my fingernails, which are rising above the bed, seem to be leaking fluid. I think they're infected. UGH.

Your takeaway: You WILL get through this. You WILL have challenges along the way. Don't obsess over them. Just keep on moving!

25

Sand, Margaritas and Nails

"This summer's gonna hurt like a mother$#@!"--"This Summer's Gonna Hurt Like a Mother…"

BY *MAROON 5*

One of the things that got me through treatment was simply to live from treatment to treatment. My life really became focused on three-week increments.

During that summer, I wasn't about to cancel plans I had.

One included a trip with my boyfriend to The Greenbrier resort in W.V., for his work convention. I had never been there and heard it was wonderful.

We went. It was.

Of course, that was after the fourth treatment, which seemed to hit me hardest. I had a horrid rash on my face, which I managed to cover up (thank you, Clinique!) and my leg muscles weren't quite up to par and it was ridiculously hot out, which with the wig, made my head itch.

But I sucked it up and enjoyed the trip, even managing to beat the BF at a clay pigeon shoot!

Best of all, I don't think anyone there knew what I was going through other than a couple at our table with whom I shared my journey, as I knew them.

As if that wasn't a little too much to have taken on, the day after we returned, my daughter and I left for our planned trip to the beach.

Overall, we had a great time.

But again, the heat was bothersome and walking through the dry sand towards the ocean with my crazy legs wasn't fun.

Also, trying to eat seafood was no fun when everything tastes "off."

I rarely ever drink, but my daughter had recently turned 21 and, well, the margarita's looked delightful! One thing I did learn is alcohol tastes pretty much the same as it always does and the buzz took the edge off the chemo buzz I had. (This is not an endorsement for drinking liquor. If you choose to drink, please do so responsibly. And always check with your doctor before adding alcohol to your treatment plan.)

In case you are curious, yes, you can wear a wig on the beach! I did. I just washed it out when I got back to the hotel.

I mean, seriously, I had to venture onto the sand in my woman-over-40 body. That was bad enough! There was no way I was going out bald.

It's funny how this experience really does change how you look at things.

I sat in the beach chair on the same beach my family visited when my daughter was little and watched young moms with their children and wondered what the future has in store for them. Never in a million years would I have guessed as I built sand castles with my young daughter that I'd be going through this a decade or two later.

I watched the surf roll in and the tide move out and thought about how lucky I was that I had this time with my daughter; how lucky I was that my cancer was caught early. I prayed that it doesn't return before my grandchildren are grown.

I know that's a lot to ask.

Meanwhile, I began to notice my fingernails were sore. I had been warned I might lose the nails, but was hoping that wouldn't be the case.

By the time I returned from the shore, my fingernails were worse.

The first thing I noticed was they had red lines on them, sort of like red moons. Then, they began to turn white and lift from the nail bed. Then, they began oozing yellow liquid and, not to gross you out, but it smelled like something found dead on the beach. Disgusting!

Assuming it was an infection, the doctor prescribed a topical cream until the culture would show us a result.

As it turned out, the culture was "normal" and I discovered that's just part of the decay process. When the nail loosens, it starts to pull away from the bed and I guess that starts to decay, because once the nail actually lifts off the surface of the finger, it stops oozing (and if you look at the fingertip, you can actually see a space between skin and nail) and at that point, the odor and ooze is gone.

My nails didn't all do this at the same time, so it took more than 3 weeks before I had no oozing. It was gross.

Speaking of things that one doesn't normally speak of, the extreme constipation I was suffering after each chemo treatment took its toll on my body as well.

In addition to the antibiotic cream for the fingernails, I began carrying Preparation H wherever I went. Nothing says "single woman" like a purse full of that!

Your takeaway: Don't let your life stop. Just take it easy. Pay attention to your body. It will tell you when you're trying to do too much. And anytime something strange or uncomfortable occurs, always run it past your doctor. Relief could be right around the corner!

26

Radiation – Or as I Liked to Think of It: Snorkeling Practice

*"I feel it in my bones enough to make my systems blow.
Welcome to the new age, to the new age
Welcome to the new age, to the new age. Whoa, whoa, I'm radioactive, radioactive
Whoa, whoa, I'm radioactive, radioactive."*

—"Radioactive" by Imagine Dragons

In order to start radiation, I was required to make an appointment for a "simulation." The last time I had participated in a "simulation," it was tenth grade driver's ed class and I got carsick.

A nurse named Doris took me back to a room, the center of which had a big CT scan machine. The first item of business was to hand me a plastic hose and teach me to breathe.

I have a very hard time breathing through my mouth, so this was going to be challenging.

Not to worry! They have a nose clip to prevent you from breathing!

A computer was hooked up to track my breathing pattern. Despite my concerns, apparently, I have a perfect breathing pattern for this sort of thing. (Who knew?!)

After I mastered that, they laid me down, hands above head, and marked a few spots on my skin with a permanent marker.

Doris then "made a mold" so that my arms would be comfortable above my head.

Worried about my left arm's comfort, she readjusted me.

I didn't have the heart to tell her it was way more comfortable the first time.

She handed me what I think was the buzzer for "Jeopardy!" and then, I was slid into the machine for a practice session (which was to make sure they marked me correctly).

Buzzer? Check.

Nose plug? Check.

Plastic breathing tube in place? Check.

I had to breathe a couple times, then hold my breath for 13.5 seconds (which seemed a heck of a lot longer than it was, possibly because they shut off the air in the hose).

Next, they slid me out of the machine and proceeded to mark me some more, this time, with tattoos—yes, ink on a needle inserted under my skin. Three spots: center of chest, under right ribcage and under left ribcage.

It didn't really hurt. Just pinched a big.

Note to self: That tattoo I wanna get? It will NOT go anywhere near my ribcage!

Next, I was told to get dressed and she'd meet me at the desk with my treatment schedule.

You'd think the scheduling would've been the easiest part of the appointment. Not so!

Doris asked which day of the week I planned to take off work for the first appointment.

"None," I replied. "It's only, what, an hour tops, I will come on my lunch hour."

I may have been mistaken, but I don't think Doris liked that answer.

She said the first appointment is always scheduled around 11:30 a.m. (which happens to be perfect for my lunchtime) and that subsequent appointments would either be 11 or earlier or after 1.

I requested 11 a.m. daily, so as not to disrupt my work schedule too much.

But when Doris returned, all she handed me was a card with my FIRST appointment on it. The remainder would be scheduled when I got there.

What the heck? I was there with my calendar and her calendar. Why not schedule all the appointments?

Are they afraid I'm not going to go through with treatment? Or is there a chance I might spontaneously combust in the machine?

How was I supposed to live my life with the least amount of disruption if I can't schedule in advance?!

This did not give me confidence.

In short order, I returned for my first radiation treatment.

Technicians Josh and Kristy lined me up on a table with the radiation machine above me.

The lining up part took surprisingly long, as they had to get me centered correctly, using my new tiny tattoos to guide them.

Because I was doing breathing therapy as part of the treatment, I had a breathing tube like a snorkel in my mouth and a nose clip on. They handed me the Jeopardy button to press and hold so that if I had a problem, I was to let go of the button and they would respond immediately.

As I lay there, Josh, provided instructions (in his very soothing radio announcer voice) over the loudspeaker, "take 2 normal breaths … first one … second one … now breathe in and hold …"

and then he counted down the number of seconds I needed to hold my breath.

For my treatment, we did that three times on one side, then the machine moved over me and we did that three times on the other side.

Then, Josh assured me I could "breathe normally."

I had to laugh. Did he forget my nose was clipped shut and I had a tube shoved in my mouth and was producing copious amounts of saliva. There was NO WAY I was going to breath normally!

From the time I hopped onto the table, it took no more than 10 minutes, usually less than five.

I felt nothing.

Breathing through the tube was the most difficult for me, as I'm not a mouth-breather, but after Day 2, I felt comfortable.

I was told there should be no side effects for at least the first couple of weeks. Why then, did I return to work and my boob itched? And then the other side itched. And then I itched all over the more I thought about it. Psychosomatic, I presume.

The radiation continued every weekday for an entire month.

I had some minor itching and burning that a little Aquaphor took care of, but nothing more. I was very fortunate.

You might think baring your boob every day to a male radiologist would be uncomfortable, but at some point, you get used to it.

But when you decide you aren't there long enough to bother with putting your shirt and bra in a locker before changing into the hospital shirt, and opt instead to carry your bra wrapped up in your shirt in with you and place on a chair, it is rather embarrassing when your black lace bra slips out of the shirt pile and lands at the male tech's feet as he follows you out of the room.

Fortunately, he took it in stride and seemed not to notice as I quickly bent down and scooped it up.

Hey, I was just grateful that I still needed a bra!

Four weeks into radiation (and now it's October and Breast Cancer Awareness Month), I offered to allow a local news crew to film me during radiation.

I did this not because I wanted publicity (in fact, I hate being in front of any kind of camera), but because talk of "radiation" is so frightening, yet the process is quite painless, I wanted to show women that.

So abc27 Daybreak's anchor Ali Lanyon and cameraman Kyrie George followed me on crisp October morning. Thank goodness, I knew both of them and was comfortable.

Poor Josh and Kristy, they knew we were coming, but didn't know my entourage would want them on camera, too!

Of course, they couldn't film while I was getting cooked (by the radiation, not to be confused with getting "baked," which would have been preferable).

So we staged it.

So I had to lay under the radiation machine, in the dark, breathing through a tube, as a cameraman filmed me.

Thank God, I knew Kyrie and was comfortable with him.

As I said, it's not a frightening process and I wanted women to understand that.

After several weeks of regular radiation, I was down to my last week.

In my case, they called it the "boost" and it focused directly on my breast scar tissue and surrounding area.

That meant I got to try a new radiation machine.

I had to go get fitted for this treatment, too, with Doris, who I'd really come to like.

She had me all lined up on the machine and needed to have the doctor "mark" me, she said.

I assumed, since she was getting a doctor to do that, that this marking process must be some big deal.

My usual doctor was on vacation, so a Dr. Frederick Newton came in.

He walked up, introduced himself. He then ever so gently removed the drape from across my chest.

I told him I'm so comfortable flashing my boobs to strange men now that I really should plan to attend Mardi Gras and score me some serious beads.

He chuckled and took a black Sharpie marker and drew a circle around my scar.

"Wow. My 5-year-old niece could've done that yesterday," I told him, "But I guess that's why they're paying you the big bucks."

He smiled and nodded as he left the room.

And that was it! That's all the marking entailed.

At this point, I had no severe burning, although I did have some redness under my arm and under my breast.

Luckily, even as I finished treatment, had no severe burning of my skin or real complications.

Your takeaway: Radiation isn't bad at all. Just think of it as another step in the journey that, hopefully, we be completed soon enough. And maybe plan a trip somewhere to celebrate when it's over. Might I suggest Mardi Gras?

27

Speaking Out—And Falling In

"Time on my side, I got it all. I've heard that pride always comes before a fall."

—"Love Is Like Oxygen" by Sweet

A colleague of mine is a morning news anchor at WHTM abc27, our local abc affiliate, and so I agreed to be on her morning program to share my message that women MUST get mammograms.

I figured if I can convince just one reluctant woman and save one life, it was worth getting out of bed well before dawn.

That morning, I left the house several hours before my normal departure time. It was still dark. I proceeded onward as I usually do on my way to work. I got about eight miles down the road before I realized I was headed toward my office out of habit, not toward the TV station.

I made a quick U-turn on the rural road I was on, headed toward the interstate and was fortunate that traffic on the highway was cruising along beyond the posted speed limit.

I made it to the station by my goal time, parked and headed toward the door.

I knew from past experience that at that time of the morning, there is no receptionist, so you have to go to the back door and ring the bell to be buzzed in.

As I headed toward the door, I could see it was under construction—big orange mesh fence surrounded the whole rear of building.

I walked around to the front main entrance—which I knew was typically dark and locked at that time of day—and looked for a buzzer.

There wasn't one.

Had I been at my desk the day before instead of out on assignment, I'd have seen the email from the anchor instructing me to call a number when I arrived, but I never thought to check my email before I left the house.

I figured the general station number would go to a reception voicemail and that's all I had.

So …

I climbed the orange fence! (Fortunately, I was wearing pants and low heels.)

I made my way to the station's back door and realized there was a three-foot hole in front of it.

I instantly knew not much good was going to come of this adventure, but I leaned over the hole to press the doorbell. As I leaned back, I accidentally slipped into the hole.

I could imagine few things worse than having some famous TV news person open the door, only to see me stuck in a dirt hole, so I quickly pulled myself up and out just before a guy named Derek opened the door, looking confused.

"Um, this entrance is under construction, you'll have to go around to the front and ring the bell," he said.

"There is no bell at the front," I replied.

We debated this fact a time or two and he assured me he'd meet me out front, so I turned, climbed back over the fence and walked around to the front.

I'm sure they have all this on security camera, I just hope no one ever finds it! I'm also fairly certain there was much conversation about my pre-dawn trip through their construction zone.

I got to the front door (checked again for a bell—there was none) where the news director was now waiting, followed by Derek.

"Yeah, there's no bell," I said to Derek.

Ready to prove me crazy (like he needed to after the back door debacle), he went outside to look for the missing doorbell.

"Wow. There isn't one," he admitted.

I felt relieved because I'd have been mortified if there was a bell somewhere I missed and trekked through the dirt for nothing.

Turns out the bell is between two sets of glass doors and both sets of doors were locked.

"You're the first person to tell me that," he said. (Yes, well I'm pretty sure I am also the only person to do an in-depth investigation around the studio and through a construction zone, too.)

I walked through the studio wondering how other morning guests found their way inside.

The interview went well, I thought, and morning anchors Ali Lanyon and James Crummel (I call him "Sweet Baby James") were fantastic as always.

I had a treatment afterwards, so when I got to the center, the nurse made mention of my TV appearance and quipped, "If the paparazzi is waiting for you at the front door, we'll let you leave through the back door."

She didn't notice me cringe ever-so-slightly at the mention of a back door!

28

Odds ... and Ends

"It's a marathon, not a sprint!"

—A*NONYMOUS*

Oh, how I hate that phrase! I ran cross country briefly in high school. In an entire season of 3.1-mile races, I quickly determined I prefer a sprint to a marathon.

Throughout my cancer journey, I kept waiting to return to "normal"—whatever that was or is anymore.

Every time I had a new appointment, be it doctor or dentist or eye doctor, I dreaded going. Even when I didn't truly dread it, my body thought I did and my pulse and blood pressure would skyrocket.

Anytime I got sick, be it a stomachache, rash or headache, I was convinced I was dying.

Throughout my year-long adventure, a lot of things irritated or amused me along the way. Mostly irritated, but I tried to find humor in them.

After the lingerie email that I had to unsubscribe from, you'd have thought I would have unsubscribed from other daily emails that had the potential to remind of me something I didn't want to be reminded about. But no.

One day, about halfway through treatment, CVS pharmacy sent me a coupon customized "just for me." It was for shaving products.

Clearly, CVS didn't really know me at all. I really missed shaving my legs. It was a chore I always looked upon with disgust, but by this point, I sure did miss it.

Next came the wonderment I met with at certain doctor appointments. The Penn State medical system was very good at being discreet with information. Other medical facilities weren't.

I was always amazed with all the HIPAA laws that required me to fill out endless paperwork that is supposed to be designed to protect my personal information, I would approach a medical reception desk and either A: was required to write down my first and last name, along with my appointment time on a clipboard for the world to see; or B: the receptionist would ask my name and date of birth, which I was supposed to state loud enough she (and anyone waiting in line or standing at the adjacent receptionist) could hear and then, she would rattle off, "I have your address as (reads address) and phone number as (reads phone number)." Some receptionists were louder than others, trust me.

Now the entire waiting room knows my birth date and where I reside. How is that protecting my personal information?!

And then there was the conversation with the medical billing company.

When I had the genetic testing done, I was warned that it may or may not be covered by insurance. They thought, since my grandmother had ovarian cancer, that the test would be covered.

The test was done in March.

The insurance company sent me a check in May with a statement saying that I *may* receive a bill.

I waited for a bill from the testing company until October and, since I didn't receive one and seven months had passed since I had the test, I assumed I was not going to be charged, so I used the insurance money to pay on my hospital bills.

In mid-December, I received a bill from the testing company. DECEMBER—nine months after the test! Were they even serious?

I called the company to set up a payment plan. The woman who barely spoke English in the billing dept told me I had several payment options, depending on how long I wanted to pay, ranging from three to 12 months. We settled on 12, figuring I could hopefully pay it off faster, but just in case ….

She then asked for my credit card number. Seriously?! If I had a credit card with an available balance, surely, I'd use it! But I don't, hence the request for a payment plan.

She then put me on hold for seven minutes before returning to inform me I could make payments via Paypal. I don't use Paypal.

"Can't I just send you a check each month" I asked. I was put on hold again. Another seven minutes later, she returned. Yes, I could mail a monthly check, she said.

Another cancer battle. Now why was that so difficult? What on earth do elderly people and others like me who aren't tech-friendly do in this world?

I had a follow-up visit with my surgeon and things appeared to be going well.

She said the effects of radiation can last a year and things will still be changing in there. I had no idea.

She asked a lot of questions and told me what to look for—pain that doesn't go away or gets worse and headaches and such.

Wow. I didn't want to think about that kind of thing.

That's the worst part of all this. You do what you have to do to get rid of the cancer and improve your odds of it not returning and once you cross all the hurdles, you are set free!

But then you worry, is it gonna come back? Every little ache and pain makes you wonder. That, for me, has been the most difficult part, especially being that I've always tended to worry about things like that anyhow.

I ran into my pink angel, Jennifer, as I was leaving the office.

She was there for her check-up, too.

Again, seeing a friendly face made my day!

But the fact of the matter was, although I was seeing very well, my eyes were still leaking, months after the chemo had been completed.

I consulted with an ophthalmologist who wanted to make sure my problem wasn't due to a blocked or scarred tear duct.

Side note: Early on into my treatment, I met with a friend who had been through it. She had advised me to visit my ophthalmologist to find out if I should get drains inserted into my tear ducts to prevent scarring from chemo. I did go to the eye doctor. He didn't find it necessary or suggested.

Fast-forward to my still-leaking eyes.

To determine if the tear duct was, in fact, blocked or scarred, he would have to do a procedure that injected saline into my tear duct.

Sounds like no big deal, right?

Before I knew it, I was tipped back in the chair and told to look up, but keep my eyes and head still.

Have you any idea how difficult it is to keep your eyes and head still when a doctor's hand is moving toward you holding a needle and syringe?

He inserted the needle into the corner of my eye and injected saline.

I was told if it ran into my nose or down my throat, that was a good thing. It did!

It only took seconds, but it felt like minutes.

Then, it was time to do the other eye, which was better in a way because I knew what to expect, but worse because I knew what to expect.

To this day, I still have issues with my one eye. I can't say it was caused by the chemo or any follow-up medications, but I can't say it wasn't. I'm told some of the problems are due to my age, yet I'm not even 50, so I can only imagine what the future holds.

Speaking of eyes, I lost part of my eyebrows, though not until AFTER the chemo was over, which I thought was odd.

I also lost many of my eyelashes.

One year after my last surgery, I discovered that breasts can remain tender as scar tissue and nerves heal.

Meanwhile, I'm still working out twice a week to strengthen my muscles and keep my joints moving.

I'm still pretty stiff and sore from time to time, which they say could be due to the anastrozole I take daily.

I could change my medication, but at this point, I can manage the symptoms. If that changes, perhaps I will switch.

I did opt for a total hysterectomy, which was truly painless. I figured that would help reduce the amount of estrogen left in my body and would, hopefully, prevent any other problems from cropping up later.

Digestive issues were also a concern for a while, even four months after I finished chemo and radiation. I think that was just my system getting used to real food again, as my diet during chemo was limited.

I also began carrying a knife with me because I found since my thumbnails separated from the nail bed (I never did lose them entirely), little things like peeling fruit became impossible. Ditto peeling labels and opening bottles and such.

There was also the follow-up where they checked my blood count and it came back wonky.

I panicked, of course.

I cried.

My oncologist was kind enough to rerun the test, because she thought it odd, too.

Fortunately, it was a bad draw.

But another panic!

Despite the negative things that happened along the way, there were many great things, too.

Leaving the hospital one day, I ran into a woman I used to attend church with. I hadn't seen her in years and there she was, standing at the door of the medical center as I was leaving.

It's a big hospital in a town 40 minutes from my town, so I'm always surprised to run into people I know.

But there she was. We chatted. She promised to add me to her prayer chain. Thanks, Rosemary! Good to catch up with you!

Your takeaway: There will always be ups and downs. Some things will shake you, some will surprise you. Learn to roll with it. It really is a marathon, not a sprint. Embrace the good things about your new life. Let go of the negative. Trust your journey!

29

Finding faith

"I can do all things through Christ who strengthens me."

—Philippians *4:13*

I have always been a spiritual person, though not always a religious person. I was raised in the church, suffered through Sunday school and, thanks to my grandmother, always had a relationship with God.

As I said before, I was never afraid to pray for whatever I thought I needed.

But what I learned through all this is God really does answer prayer. It may not be the answer you were expecting or you may not get what you want in the way you wanted it, but you will get your blessing.

As I mentioned before, I asked God for patience. I asked him for good friends. And I don't recall ever really praying for thicker hair and perkier boobs, but I know I sure coveted them!

After my divorce, I asked Him to fix what was wrong with me that prevented me from having a healthy, loving relationship.

I wanted less anger and more patience. I wanted to find happiness. I wanted to appreciate what I had.

Now, here I am, and I realize I have been given all those things.

You see, without the cancer, I never would have changed. Oh, I would have probably been more patient—for a day, maybe two.

I would have dropped my unrealistic expectations of my partner for a weekend.

I would have stopped being angry on Sundays, maybe.

And I would have continued to look ahead, waiting for the next better thing to cross my path, be it a better car or a better house or a trip or whatever the next "get" was.

That's just how I rolled and I'm sad that I lived like that.

But now, thanks to my cancer journey, I am reminded every day to live for today.

I know for certain tomorrow is not promised. I have seen behind the curtain.

I have learned there are some things I can control, but many things I cannot.

I have learned to appreciate more and demand less.

And I have learned how to love and accept love in a much healthier way.

Don't get me wrong, not everything is perfect. There are still a few wounds to be healed.

And, sure, I slip now and then. I still get angry from time to time. I still get caught in the "I want…" loop.

But then I look at my scars and I remember that I am lucky to be alive.

And I thank God every day for the opportunity to live another day!

I have seen so many things through this journey that I know are God. I could tell you a dozen stories about my faith walk, but not everyone is a believer, so I will keep them to myself for now. But if you're curious, ask me!

I am blessed.

Your takeaway: Stay true to your system of beliefs, whatever that system is.

There are blessings in your journey, too, whatever that journey may be. This, I know! Just be open and look for them.

30

--30--

"And we'll all float on OK!"

—*"Float On" by Modest Mouse*

In journalism, "30" is what reporters used to type at the end of their stories to indicate the end of the story. We don't do it anymore. Occasionally, you'll see it done in a press release, but that's generally how you know that whoever is writing that release is old enough to know what they are doing and is serious about whatever event they are writing about, so you'd better take note.

According to the American Journalism Review, one theory as to why this was done suggests that the first telegraphed news story had 30 words. Another theory suggests the numeral stems back to a time when stories were written in longhand and an "X" marked the end of a sentence, an "XX" indicated the end of a paragraph and "XXX" meant the end of the story and "XXX" in Roman numerals translates to "30."

At any rate, this is the end of my story. At least I hope it is the end of my cancer journey, although the journey never really ends.

My life has changed forever.

But I've seen some things come full circle.

After my year-long Herceptin treatment, I finally had Obama deported.

It took nearly 40 minutes and two nurses to find a proper vein to insert the IV, but the third stick was the charm.

Like during the insertion, I was awake, but not really aware of what was going on. It's an odd state.

What was strange was I was awake and normal and the nurse said she was going to give me something to relax and all of a sudden, my chest felt like I had the wind knocked out of me and then I felt my head get "funny."

I realized I rather liked that feeling, so I suppose that's how people get addicted to drugs.

But it's sure not something I'd want to mess with!

Again, I got my classic itchy red rash where the bandage adhesive was afterwards and that was one of the worst parts to every surgery I had.

Unlike his namesake, I wanted to keep this Obama as a memento, but hospital safety practices prevented me from taking him home.

The nurse was kind enough to take a photo of the port for me as my souvenir.

Recovery ended with the best chicken salad sandwich I think I ever ate, and vegetable soup, plus fruit and a S'mores dessert. I felt so spoiled!

Since that last surgery more than a year ago, (I bear the scar on my chest), my new normal has begun to blend with my old normal.

My eyelashes are almost all grown back. They are still very short, but I can finally get a mascara wand to reach all of them.

My eyebrows have returned.

I've gotten my hair trimmed and colored.

Two of my fingernails are still dead and discolored and I have to keep them short or they catch on things, but the rest have grown out. But even two years later, I'm still battling with in-grown and infected fingernails due to regrowth.

I've had some vision problems with floaters that they tell me could be caused by either the drastic and sudden drop in estrogen in my body or it could be a side effect of the estrogen-blocking medication I take daily.

I still have some muscle weakness in my legs that as long as I continue to work out regularly at the gym, I don't notice.

The most interesting thing since then is I have a hard time regulating my body temperature, especially if the room temperature changes even slightly. I am always cold.

I guess that's the lack of estrogen.

I have found sugar gives me hot flashes. Seriously, give me a sugared beverage or a dessert and in about 10 to 20 minutes, I will be peeling off layers of clothing.

It's funny how since I discovered it is the sugar doing it, the hot flashes have been eliminated.

I do feel like a little old lady sometimes!

But there are always positives, too.

I always said I wanted to reach one person through my journey. And I did.

Along the way, I met my friend, Michele. Our paths initially crossed due to my job.

I was to interview her daughter for the magazine and had to call her house and let a message.

Michele got my message and, long story short, recognized my name as the author of the article she recently read about my breast cancer.

At the time, she, too, had been just diagnosed. We were about the same age. She had been meaning to contact me to thank me for sharing my story, as it was something she could relate to.

We became fast friends and I simply adore her.

She calls me her "cancer angel."

I don't take that role lightly as I know exactly what that means to someone who is going through this.

I am thankful to be for her what Jennifer was for me.

I think that's so cool how that worked!

I hope we will continue to be friends for many years to come, but even if we grow apart due to our busy lives, we will always have a special place in each other's heart.

Throughout most of my journey, I was very opposed to shouting to the world that I had breast cancer through pink ribbon pins and jewelry. At the time, I just wanted to forget. I just wanted to be normal.

But I changed my mind after encountering the woman in the airport. I'd never have met her and made her my mentor for living had she not had a keychain on her totebag.

Since then, I try to wear a bracelet or sport something with a pink ribbon daily, because maybe someone going through breast cancer treatment will spot it and feel comfortable to ask me questions. Or maybe I will meet a survivor. I figure if I tend to now look for those telltale signs, others do, too.

I understand not everyone has what I call the "journalist's nerve" to approach someone and ask questions, but if that opens the door to one curious survivor or victim, I am there to help!

It really is a club. It's a club we all wish we didn't belong to, but we all need support.

It's great to have family and friends who stand by you, but they can't really comprehend what you are going through unless they have been through it, too.

Speaking of support, my boyfriend stood by me through all my treatment and is now my husband. I knew he was a keeper when we met, but anybody who stands by and manages to support you while making life "normal" is clearly in love and I sure do love him for it.

And finally, I had my one-year follow-up and mammogram, which I dreaded to the point of not being able to sleep for days leading up to it.

I had minor panic attacks.

I cried.

I thought I'd actually have to take one of those Ativans that I had a prescription for, but I opted not to take it and instead, turned to a prayer chain.

I was escorted back to the mammography room and the procedure was completed.

I had to wait for the results in the same waiting room I waited in many times before.

This time, the room had a picture of nature on the screen and birds flying and chirping.

Was that even serious?

Flying chirping birds?! Surely, that's just one nature scene away from buzzards circling and, well, maybe the buzzards will circle next if the cancer has returned and I'm dying!

Why can't they have HGTV on like every other office?!

I don't know what the future holds. And you know what? I'm not sure I WANT to know.

I just want to enjoy every day, every moment. I want to be able to look back and say I've enjoyed my life and appreciated my many blessings.

Of course, I want to be around a long time for my family and I have my eye on that 20-year survival mark.

But I have no control over that. I can only hope and pray and live day by day.

After what seemed like an eternity (or an entire season, as the birds eventually stopped chirping and a chorus of crickets and frogs sounded), the mammography technician returned to tell me everything was clear.

"Dr. Watts sends her regards," she said.

Annnndddd… we have come full circle!!! YAY!

Although my cancer is in remission for now, my journey doesn't end.

I now live with a constant fear that the cancer will return. If I keep busy, the little voice or "pink cloud" as some women call it, isn't as noticeable.

It hits me mostly at night or when I encounter another person with cancer or when I read the obituaries. (Yes, I need to stop doing that, but I work at a newspaper, so it's difficult to not read them).

And I carry with me some guilt, too.

Like on the days when my 20-mile drive to work takes 40 minutes because I get behind some idiot traveling 45 mph in a 55 zone or when I run to the bank at work over lunch and some clearly retired person has chosen 12:15 p.m. to go purchase $2 bills to give to the grandchildren and she has to tell the teller all about the grandkids and how old they are and their names and what they are doing in life. Seriously? You have ALL DAY to run your errands, why must you go during every working person's lunch hour?!

I get angry.

Or sometimes, I just have a bad day where my boss is an idiot and work sucks.

Those are the days when not only do I feel the emotion of the moment, but then I feel guilty because I should just be damn lucky to be alive.

That's when I sit and cry.

And then I feel guilty for crying. It's a vicious cycle—and something I struggle with regularly.

I have been told it gets better, but it never goes away.

I've come to think that's OK. I think maybe I need those feelings to remind me how blessed I really am.

I know many people do not survive this horrible disease. I know many people aren't as lucky as I was to get through treatment so effortlessly.

I don't want to take away anything from their journeys.

I pray for cancer victims every day knowing some of them won't receive healing and there really is no way I can wrap my brain around the fact that some of us survive and some don't. I don't understand. I will never understand.

But I can promise to live my life with gratitude for as long as I have life.

A few years ago, I didn't appreciate my many blessings. I took many things for granted. Still probably do.

But I have a much better perspective now and for that, I'm grateful.

Living with or through this disease is a struggle. There are so many facets to it during and after treatment. Life will truly never be the same.

But you have to accept your new "normal" (and recognize that that normal might change from week to week, month to month or year to year).

Appreciate the blessings you have in life. Love your family. Find joy where you can. And have fun!

Blessings to you.

Your takeaway: As I continue on my journey, you, too, continue on yours. I leave you with a final thought, thanks to Phil Collins:

"Turn your head and don't look back. Set your sails for a new horizon, don't turn around don't look down. Oh there's life across the tracks. And you know it's really not surprising, it gets better when you get there."

WHAT NO ONE TELLS YOU

"Nobody told me there'd be days like these. Nobody told me there'd be days like these. Nobody told me there'd be days like these. Strange days indeed."

—JOHN LENNON

There are things about this journey nobody mentions until something happens. I think the doctors and nurses do that intentionally so as not to stress patients or plant the seed of whatever it is into the minds of patients. I suppose that's a good strategy.

But on the other hand, I'd have liked to have known about some of these things, so that I didn't panic when something happened to me.

Here are things that nobody tells you that may (or may not) apply to you:

- Scents of things you loved will begin to turn you off. This includes lotions, soaps, etc. After the first or second treatment, I had to change fragrances of everything—and had to do so multiple times. Some smells just made me feel sick.
- Food will turn you off. They do warn you about this. But find something you can tolerate (and it may change periodically and unexpectedly). It's important to maintain a healthy diet,

but it's just as important to eat something—anything—to keep your strength up.

- If you had a regular menstrual cycle, it may change or stop. Mine stopped. You may get a yeast infection or a bacterial infection or you may just have dryness and unusual discharge. This is "normal" but unpleasant. Talk to your doctor about remedies (Replens and coconut oil were two suggested to me and both worked great).
- Your eyes may leak—one or both. People may wonder if you are crying. Your eye makeup will quickly disappear. Your under-eye skin may get red and chapped. (TIP: if this happens, apply lip balm under your eyes—the waxy, unscented kind. It works!) If this happens, please mention it to your oncologist and eye doctor. It's likely just dry eye caused by the chemo.
- Your fingernails may hurt. They may get infected. Sometimes, they may fall off. If they loosen up, you may get a putrid odor from the decay. All this is "normal." (Although make sure they test you for an infection if your nails are leaky and stinky). Also if you lose your nails, you won't be able to hook your necklaces and bracelets.
- Expect the unexpected. I got a nasty rash on my face twice during treatment. It looked something between rash from being slapped hard and a sunburn. My lips swelled a bit, too. We later attributed it to one of the chemo drugs, but in the meantime, I had redness on my face that was horrifying. I found Clinique makes a Redness Relief daily moisturizer cream that helped immensely. I used it every day (and still use it daily) under my makeup. I use their foundation as well, since it's allergy-tested and works well in conjunction with their moisturizers.

- Depending on what type of chemo you are on, you may feel bone pain. You may develop muscle weakness. Always mention anything like that to your doctor. In my case, I developed muscle weakness particularly in my right leg to the point where I could not do two flights of stairs without stopping. I started working out with a personal trainer to strengthen my muscles and it has been a Godsend. I strongly suggest regular exercise during treatment. If you find yourself weak and worried, ask about physical therapy.
- I was warned about possible diarrhea or constipation, but nobody said the constipation would be extreme. I will spare you details except to say if you are experiencing this after your first treatment and you see a commercial for "Squatty Potty," buy it!
- Speaking of things nobody wants to speak of, if you hadn't yet reached menopause at the time of your diagnosis, you can kiss your periods (and your youth) goodbye … and say hello to the problems of aging! In the middle of my treatment, I felt sore. My joints ached. Sex became painful. This is the new normal, I was told. I was 46 when diagnosed but within a few short months, I felt like I should start lunching at the local senior center. Although I was nearly of age, I wasn't in menopause before chemo. The chemo put me into menopause. My skin got very dry. Did I mention even sex hurt? I now know why they call it "menopause"—because you have to put your man on "pause" until you figure out a way to make intimacy not hurt! (I am thinking The Snarky Girl's Guide to Menopause" will be my sequel!) Nobody warned me about this. It is not uncommon. The good news is, there is treatment available. "It's a quality-of-life issue," my doctor explained. Yes, indeed! You lose your boob (or part of it), lose your hair, lose your sense of self, lose your dreams and lose

some of your sanity, and THEN discover you've lost your pleasure, too. And doesn't that just hit below the belt?!
- Apparently, once you have cancer and/or chemo, you become like the taboo tiki the "Brady Bunch" kids found in Hawaii—nobody wants to touch you because they are afraid you'll bring back luck. Months after my chemo ended, my new dentist required a release form signed by my oncologist that I was OK to have my teeth cleaned. My massage therapist also asked me for a form. I know all cancer cases and treatments are different, but wow, that seems a little over-cautious.
- Be mindful of your partner or family support people. This journey affects them, too. I have discovered it probably takes as much of a toll on your partner or primary support person as it does on you. The difference is, you are receiving treatment and taking steps to kick it. You are doing something. Your partner is standing by and can do very little as you go on. This can be difficult for those who love you. They want to do something, but don't know what to do. Don't deprive them of helping. Tell them what they can do to make it better for you. Give them a job. Help them help you!

My tips:

- Have a wig ready, even if you decide not to wear it. Ditto scarves or some other head covering. The American Cancer Society offers a wig program and www.tlcdirect.org has a variety of styles and colors at very reasonable prices. Your wigs are generally considered a prosthetic when it comes to insurance, so often, they are covered. Check with your doctor or insurance company about that.

- Yes, you CAN wear a wig to bed! I didn't think to do this until almost done with treatment, but wish I would've sooner. I bought two of the same style so one was for bedtime (and to stuff in my purse when I rode the motorcycle in case we stopped and I wanted hair), the other for daytime/work.
- If you are a believer, get on a prayer chain. This is helpful both because you have a bunch of people (who want to help, but don't know how) praying for you and if you do one through social media, you have the opportunity to pray for others who are going through tough times, too. I found it extremely beneficial.
- Let your support system be a support system if they offer (and sometimes, even if they don't). This was my most difficult challenge (aside from losing my hair). You don't need to do it all yourself. I value my strength and independence and I CAN do almost everything. But by doing so, I shut out many people who love me and wanted to help or just be there for me and I denied them of that. Sometimes, it's not about you. Friends will want to help. Let them.
- Stay in shape. Cancer treatment is expensive even with insurance, so joining a gym may not be feasible, but you MUST stay active. I intended to walk every day, but I got lazy after the first week. I had weakness in my legs after chemo, not to mention edema. It was causing me difficulties walking, especially on the stairs. I was lucky and found a personal trainer who worked with me post-treatment. My advice is pick one of those friends who has offered to help. Pick the most persistent/annoying/enthusiastic/honest of them and ask her to be your "trainer" by holding you accountable to exercise. If she can do it with you, great! If not, at least have her check in daily and ask if you exercised (and not accept your excuses for doing nothing).

- Always talk to your doctor. Ask as many questions as you need, whenever you need to. Information on the internet is often misleading, confusing and, I found, downright negative. There were so many cancer communities where people posted about awful side effects and all kinds of negative things. You don't need that. Think about it: Most people who take the time to post anything are often disgruntled or just negative. Rarely do you find the good stuff.
- If you have swelling and lymphedema issues—even minor ones, talk to your doctor about compression stockings and wraps. They work wonders!
- Live your life. Enjoy things. Do things when you feel up to it.
- Yes, you can ride go-karts or a motorcycle. Always wear a helmet. Don't wear a wig under your helmet, use a scarf or do-rag. One thing that kept life normal during my summer of treatments was to take the motorcycle out for a spin on the weekends. When I was sitting on the back sporting the helmet, I forgot all about not having hair.
- Before your first treatment—and during—drink lots of water. Buy a new travel mug or cup and fill it multiple times each day. Water is best, but if you can't stand the taste (I couldn't after a while) drink 100 percent juice or whatever else you can tolerate. Hydration is key!
- Don't try to eat anything you really enjoy during chemo. My guilty pleasure was always a strawberry-frosted Dunkin' Donut. I avoided them during my entire treatment because I didn't want to ruin them forever. But food was a problem for me during treatment. So many things turned me off. Oddly, I found one thing I was able to eat consistently throughout treatment: An Arby's roast beef. Fortunately, there was a restaurant not far from my office and I would go at least once a

week and enjoy a lunch. I added in an orange cream shake and it was almost divine! It probably wasn't the healthiest thing, but it was the only meal I knew would settle without issue.
- Keep an extra makeup bag in your desk at work or your car or purse or wherever, because you will probably need to reapply makeup throughout the day, especially eye makeup. I was lucky and didn't lose my eyelashes until after the fifth treatment (and then, only some of them). Eyeliner and shadow was key to looking and feeling pretty. I found the IT Cosmetics universal brow power eye brow pencil to be worth its weight in gold for creating/filling in eyebrows. I didn't use mascara during treatment, but afterwards, what little lashes I had left, I tried to find the mascara with the tiniest brush I could to catch those little lashes.
- If you are having radiation, find a deodorant with no aluminum. You'll probably be required to use it. Arm & Hammer offers one that works quite well. Also, take a look at all your beauty products. Now might be a good time to ditch anything with parabens in it. I didn't opt to go all-natural, but I have cut back on those with lots of ingredients. For me, soap was the easiest place to start. I found a local woman who makes the most luxurious soaps using natural ingredients and none of the icky stuff. Her name is Kalpana. You can find her online at kalpanasfinesoaps.com.

A NOTE TO FRIENDS AND FAMILY: DOS AND DON'TS
Feel free to copy this list and send it to family members or post on social media, with credit to The Snarky Girl's Guide to Breast Cancer.

WHAT NOT TO DO:
Don't look at me with that slight head tilt and sad, teary eyes as if you believe I'm dying. I'm not—yet at least. And hey, we're

all dying. Technically, we've been dying since the day we were born and none of us can stop it. I'm no different than I was a few weeks or months ago, I just happened to be getting treated now.

Don't call me every darned day to see how I'm doing. I have good days and bad days. On the good days, I don't want to be reminded by your call that anything is wrong. On bad days, I will call you if I need to talk. Let me lead.

If you didn't refer to me by terms of endearment before, please don't start now. "Hi, honey/sweetheart" only makes me feel like a child who is in need of something. And it sounds condescending and disingenuous.

And really, for the love of all that's right in the world, don't look at me and cry. I mean, seriously?! Believe me, I've shed enough tears to fill the jetted garden tub I lost in my divorce, I don't need to see you cry.

WHAT YOU CAN DO TO HELP:
Here are things that would have helped me greatly:

Give a giftcard. It's nice to stop for a special treat after stressful appointments and cash is a rare commodity for many of us with staggering medical bills. Even $5 cards for places like Starbucks or Dunkin Donuts or Sheetz would be great. And restaurant giftcards would be nice, too, because in my case, a lot of food turned me off during chemo. I couldn't stand to cook because by the time the food was prepared, it turned my stomach. But there were things I craved from time to time or found "safe" in that it didn't turn my stomach. Giftcards are perfect for that.

Offer a meal. Whether you cook it and drop it off or you offer to bring take-out or provide a dinner invitation, this, too, helps. Sometimes it's less about the food and more about the company; other times, it's all about the food!

Plan an outing. Invite your cancer patient out to do something fun. Of course, there may be limits, so don't make it too stressful, but just a ride to a pretty spot or a trip to a local mall or book talk or concert keeps life normal. Don't plan any expensive trip or event because it may end up being a bad day, but little things are great distractions.

Do a household chore. There's always something, whether dishes or laundry or cleaning a bathroom or mowing the yard or shoveling snow that needs done around the house and chemo patients aren't always up to these things. In my case, it was less about the chore and more about the smell of soaps and cleaners that turned me off. But I sure appreciated it when some mystery neighbor shoveled or mowed my yard.

Be a shoulder to cry on. Sometimes, you just need to throw a pity party and you want a good friend there. Just be there to listen.

Gift some bling! During treatment, my fingernails loosened from the nail beds, which meant I could no longer hook my necklaces and bracelets. A friend had no idea this happened, but coincidentally, sent me an elastic bracelet which provided much-needed bling! My boyfriend bought me a necklace that was long enough to go over my head and could easily be adjusted so I didn't need to worry about the clasp. Jewelry is one thing that makes you feel normal or pretty. To think that I couldn't wear mine was just another blow.

Gift some soaps, lotions or beauty items. As I mentioned, the smell of things turned me off and it changed on a weekly basis. One week, a lotion smelled great, but the next, it turned my stomach. Toothpaste was another thing that did that. Many of these items are pricey and I really couldn't afford to go buy new lotion or shampoo. Even if I would have ended up with 10 bottles of half-used lotion, I could have used them after treatment ended. Note cards are another nice little gift the patient could use for writing thank-yous.

END NOTES

Thank you to the group who sewed those little round pillows for the Breast Center at Penn State Hershey Med. That was a godsend!

Thank you to Fleetwood Mac and Frank Sinatra and Ozzy Osbourne and James Ingram and all the other artists whose lyrics inspired me through my journey and the writing of this book.

To all those women who are going through cancer treatments, stay strong! Take it one day at a time!

If you enjoyed this book or it helped you get through treatment, I'd love to hear from you! Please contact me at snarkygirl1016@gmail.com or follow me on Twitter @snarkygirl1016.

www.ingramcontent.com/pod-product-compliance
Lightning Source LLC
Chambersburg PA
CBHW022109090426
42743CB00008B/782